PUBLISHER'S NOTE

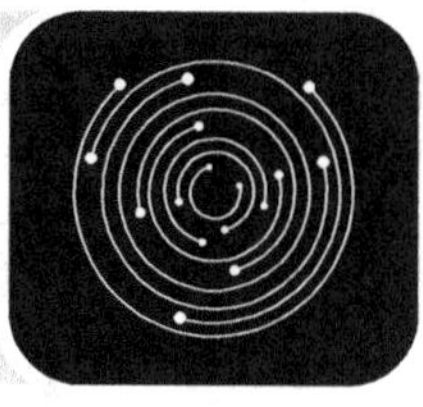

V&S Publishers has carved a significant niche in the publishing industry over the last decade, having successfully published more than 1000 titles across 9 languages spanning over 50 subject categories. Being known for the quality of content, we have built a reputation of excellence and reliability. We have consistently delivered **"Value & Substance"** to our readers, through a wide range of titles across a variety of genres covering school books, fiction and non-fiction that caters to different people from every section of the society.

The **Olympiad Guidebooks for classes 1-10** across all subjects, launched almost a decade ago, under the **GEN X Imprint**, became a go-to-source for the school students in no time, owing to their invaluable and substantive content written in a guidebook pattern,.

Having successfully sold a million copies of the same and in response to demand by both students as well as shopkeepers nationwide; we now present before you our newly launched **Olympiad Workbook Series**, designed for **classes 1-10 across 4 subjects**.

The workbooks are meticulously curated by a team of experienced educators, researchers and subject matter experts, edited by professionals and peer reviewed by teachers. The team has poured its efforts and expertise into creating a crisp and concise workbook which will help and guide the students to the path of success in Olympiad exams. The **MCQs** identified will not only help in scoring top marks in Olympiads but also inculcate a sense of deeper understanding of the subject, by way of solving **HOTS** and referring to complete solutions at the end of the book.

Here we present our new release– **OLYMPIAD WORKBOOK (IMO) CLASS–2** having following features:

- ☞ Based on the latest syllabi
- ☞ MCQs with comprehensive coverage of topics
- ☞ HOTS Questions liberally included
- ☞ A dedicated chapter on logical reasoning
- ☞ Model test paper for thorough practice
- ☞ Sample OMR sheet for real time simulation

We have made sure through our best efforts, that this workbook strictly follows the latest syllabi and patterns of the Olympiad Examination.

As **V&S Publishers** continuously strive to enhance the readability and maintain the credibility of our academic publications, we seek the support of our valuable readers in influencing and enriching the lives of future generations of students.

P.S. While every care has been taken to ensure the correctness of the content, if you come across any error, howsoever minor, do not hesitate to discuss with teachers while pointing that out to us in no uncertain terms.

We wish you all the best for your exams!

DISTINCTIVE FEATURES

01

Learning Objectives

They list the whole chapter as subtopics, helping the teachers to guide children in a step-by-step manner.

02

Multiple Choice Questions

MCQs act as an excellent learning aid, helping you to understand and work on your mistakes.

03

HOTS (Achievers Section)

The High Order Thinking Questions aim to help the student to solve Application-based questions and gain practical understanding of the subject.

04

Model Test Paper

Model test paper are provided at the end of each book, which help the student to test the knowledge which they have gained after thorough reading of all chapters.

05

Answer Key

Detailed Answer Key along with explanations aid the pupil to indentify, understand the mistakes they make during the course of Olympiad preparation.

OLYMPIAD WORKBOOK

INTERNATIONAL MATHEMATICS OLYMPIAD

- **01** Learning Objectives
- **02** Multiple Choice Questions
- **03** HOTS (Achievers Section)
- **04** Model Test Paper
- **05** Answer Keys and Solutions
- **06** OMR Answer Sheet

V&S PUBLISHERS

Published by:

V&S PUBLISHERS

F-2/16, Ansari road, Daryaganj, New Delhi-110002
☎ 23240026, 23240027 • *Fax:* 011-23240028
✉ info@vspublishers.com • ⊕ www.vspublishers.com

 **Online Brandstore: amazon.in/vspublishers**

Regional Office : Hyderabad
5-1-707/1, Brij Bhawan (Beside Central Bank of India Lane)
Bank Street, Koti, Hyderabad - 500 095
☎ 040-24737290
✉ vspublishershyd@gmail.com

Follow us on:   

BUY OUR BOOKS FROM: AMAZON   FLIPKART

© Copyright: V&S PUBLISHERS
ISBN 978-81-977325-2-2
New Edition

CONTENTS

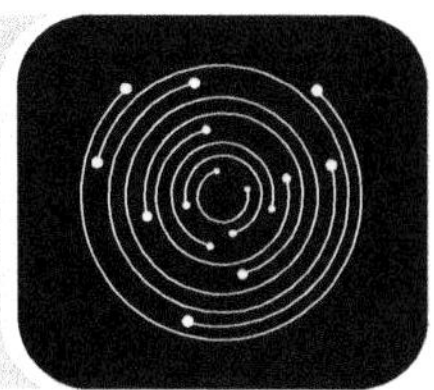

NUMBER SENSE

LEARNING OBJECTIVES

- ➤ Number System
- ➤ Place Value
- ➤ Comparing of Numbers
- ➤ Successor and Predecessor of a Number
- ➤ Odd and Even Numbers

MULTIPLE CHOICE QUESTIONS

1. The greatest 3-digit odd number is _____.
   (A) 920   (B) 925
   (C) 952   (D) 902

2. Which of the following number names does not show the number in the box?

567	221	327	999

   (A) Two hundred twenty-one
   (B) Three hundred twenty-seven
   (C) Five hundred sixty-seven
   (D) Three hundred thirty-three

3. Which number is shown on the abacus?

   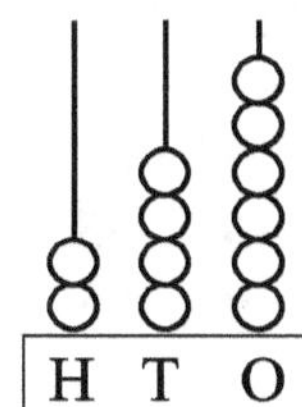

   (A) 643   (B) 246
   (C) 245   (D) 346

4. The smallest 3-digit even number is __.
   (A) 052   (B) 520
   (C) 950   (D) 250

5. Which of the following number has 3 in tens place?
   (A) 323   (B) 396
   (C) 438   (D) 943

6. The number having '3' in the hundreds place, '5' in the ones place and '2' in the tens place is ________:
   (A) 352   (B) 532
   (C) 253   (D) 325

7. Which symbol should be written in the box below to make the number sentence correct?
   432 ☐ 318
   (A) >   (B) <
   (C) =   (D) All of these

8. What number is 10 less than 205?
   (A) 215   (B) 195
   (C) 135   (D) 185

9. Which of the following statements is correct?
   (A) $321 < 235$ (B) $420 > 510$
   (C) $725 < 638$ (D) $827 > 639$

10. The smallest 3-digit number is________ :
    (A) 999   (B) 100
    (C) 1000   (D) 99

11. Find the missing number from the following:
    $$597 = 500 + \ldots\ldots \times 10 + 7$$
    (A) 597   (B) 97
    (C) 90   (D) 9

12. Write down the numbers from 1 to 25 one after the other. Which digit is on the 25th place?
(A) 7   (B) 5
(C) 3   (D) 1

13. The greatest even number formed by the digits 3, 2 and 1 using only once is______.
(A) 321   (B) 312
(C) 213   (D) 132

14. Which of the following is the predecessor of 390?
(A) 389   (B) 393
(C) 392   (D) 390

15. Look at these numbers :

1   3   5   7   9   2   4   6   0   8

Which number is fifth from the right?
(A) 9   (B) 5
(C) 2   (D) 4

16. Rajesh lost one of his chickens. Use the clues below to help him.

Clue 1 : The digit in the ones place is 5.

Clue 2 : The digit in the tens place is greater than the digit in the ones place.

Clue 3 : The digit in the tens place is 7 more than the digit in the hundred place.

Mark the correct chicken.

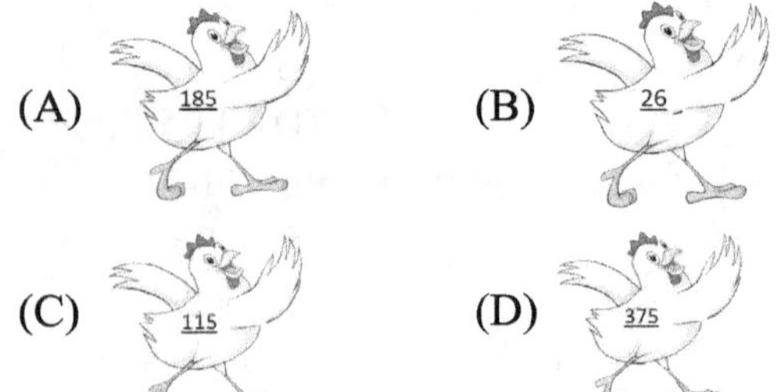

(A) 185   (B) 26
(C) 115   (D) 375

17. A boy has drawn a ball from a bag containing balls numbered from 1 to 100. It is found to be 19 more than the least two digit number. What is the number?

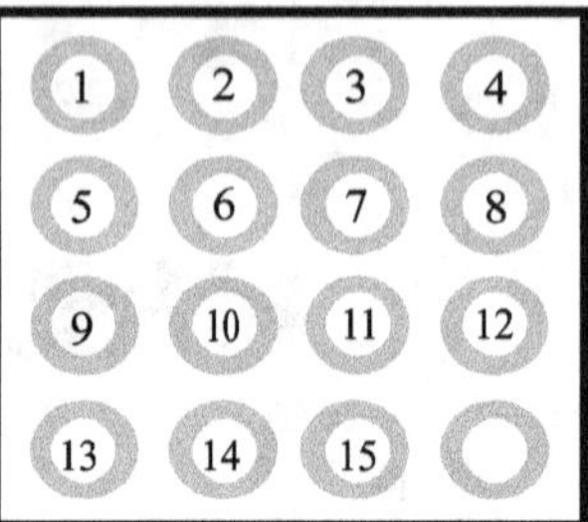

(A) 10   (B) 19
(C) 29   (D) 99

18. Golu wrote a number on the black board i.e.,

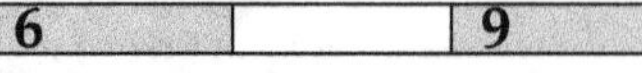

If it is formed from three different digits, then which number could be placed in the gap to make it the biggest number?
(A) 0   (B) 5
(C) 9   (D) 8

19. Golu has 387 stamps in his collection. What is 387 rounded to the nearest 10?
(A) 370   (B) 380
(C) 390   (D) 400

20. Ravi obtained 405, 365, 465, 307 and 495 marks in Class I, Class II, Class III, Class IV and Class V, respectively. He wants to arrange his marks in ascending order. What is the correct ascending order?
(A) 307, 405, 365, 465, 495
(B) 307, 365, 465, 405 , 495
(C) 307, 365, 405, 465, 495
(D) 365, 307, 405, 495, 465

OLYMPIAD WORKBOOK (IMO) CLASS– 2

21. Which of the following statement is incorrect?
    (A) There are 5 tens in 657.
    (B) The place value of 7 in 976 is 70.
    (C) 59 > 95
    (D) 80 tens is equal to 8 hundreds.

22. The number shown on the abacus is_____.

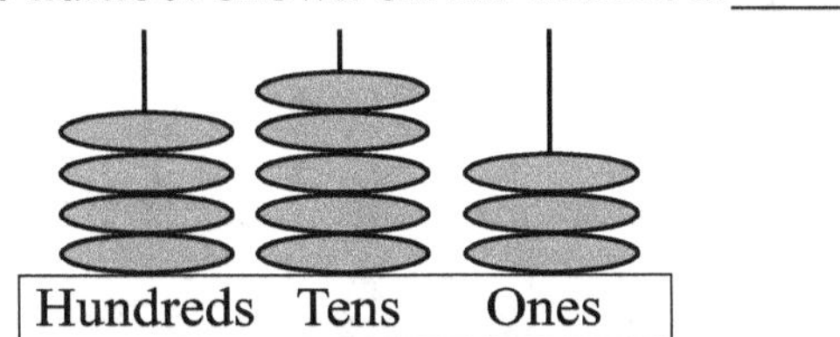

    (A) 12   (B) 400
    (C) 450   (D) 453

23. What is the expanded form of 956?
    (A) 9 Hundreds + 6 tens + 5 ones
    (B) 8 Hundreds + 9 tens + 8 ones
    (C) 9 Hundreds + 8 tens + 8 ones
    (D) 9 Hundreds + 5 tens + 6 ones

24. Fill the box.

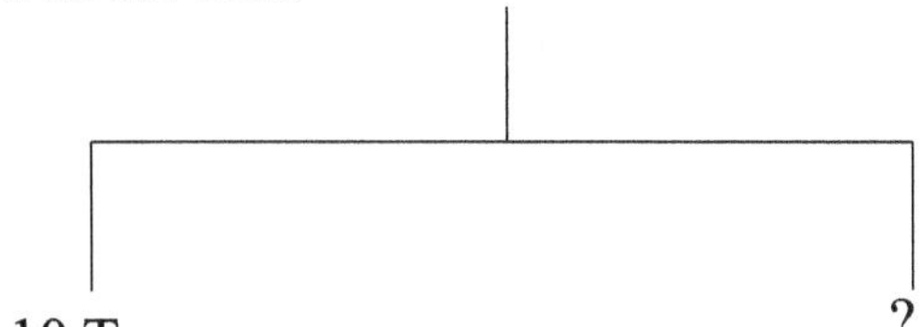

10 Tens   ?

    (A) 1 Hundred
    (B) 90 Ones
    (C) 2 Hundreds
    (D) 10 Ones

25. Read the clues and find the number.
    Clue 1: The digit at hundreds place is 2 more than the digit at ones place.
    Clue 2 : The place value of 5 is 50.
    (A) 735   (B) 975
    (C) 957   (D) 846

---

1. Ⓐ Ⓑ Ⓒ Ⓓ	6. Ⓐ Ⓑ Ⓒ Ⓓ	11. Ⓐ Ⓑ Ⓒ Ⓓ	16 Ⓐ Ⓑ Ⓒ Ⓓ	21. Ⓐ Ⓑ Ⓒ Ⓓ
2. Ⓐ Ⓑ Ⓒ Ⓓ	7. Ⓐ Ⓑ Ⓒ Ⓓ	12. Ⓐ Ⓑ Ⓒ Ⓓ	17. Ⓐ Ⓑ Ⓒ Ⓓ	22. Ⓐ Ⓑ Ⓒ Ⓓ
3. Ⓐ Ⓑ Ⓒ Ⓓ	8. Ⓐ Ⓑ Ⓒ Ⓓ	13. Ⓐ Ⓑ Ⓒ Ⓓ	18. Ⓐ Ⓑ Ⓒ Ⓓ	23. Ⓐ Ⓑ Ⓒ Ⓓ
4. Ⓐ Ⓑ Ⓒ Ⓓ	9. Ⓐ Ⓑ Ⓒ Ⓓ	14. Ⓐ Ⓑ Ⓒ Ⓓ	19. Ⓐ Ⓑ Ⓒ Ⓓ	24. Ⓐ Ⓑ Ⓒ Ⓓ
5. Ⓐ Ⓑ Ⓒ Ⓓ	10. Ⓐ Ⓑ Ⓒ Ⓓ	15. Ⓐ Ⓑ Ⓒ Ⓓ	20. Ⓐ Ⓑ Ⓒ Ⓓ	25. Ⓐ Ⓑ Ⓒ Ⓓ

ADDITION AND SUBTRACTION

LEARNING OBJECTIVES

➤ Properties of Addition

➤ Properties of Subtraction

MULTIPLE CHOICE QUESTIONS

1. $26 + 2 =$ _______ $- 3$
   (A) 24
   (B) 25
   (C) 28
   (D) 31

2. What must be added to 999 to get 1000?
   (A) 1
   (B) 101
   (C) 9001
   (D) 9999

3. $570 + 430$ is equal to how many tens?
   (A) 100
   (B) 43
   (C) 57
   (D) 1000

4. Which number should be written in the box below to make the number sentence correct?

   $20 > \square + 10$
   (A) 5
   (B) 10
   (C) 15
   (D) 20

5. Which digit should come in place of '*'?

   ```
       5      *
   +   3      8
   _____________
       9      2
   ```
   (A) 4
   (B) 3
   (C) 2
   (D) 1

6. If we add 9 tens, 5 hundreds and 3 ones then the result is:
   (A) 395
   (B) 17
   (C) 953
   (D) 593

7. If the smallest 1-digit number is added to a number, we get:
   (A) It's predecessor
   (B) 2-digit number
   (C) It's successor
   (D) Can't say

8. Add me to 6 or subtract me from 14. The answer is the same. Who am I?
   (A) 14
   (B) 10
   (C) 6
   (D) 4

9. $786 -$ _______ $= 5$ less than 116.
   (A) 675
   (B) 781
   (C) 670
   (D) 791

10. The number with more digits is _______.
    (A) Always greater.
    (B) Sometimes greater.
    (C) Always smaller.
    (D) Can't say.

11. Difference between 25 and 205 is _______.
    (A) 180
    (B) 130
    (C) 30
    (D) 230

12. 6 tens $- 4$ is equal to _______.
    (A) 64
    (B) 56
    (C) 604
    (D) 640

13. What number replace question mark to make the number sentence true?

    $40 - ? = 24$
    (A) 38
    (B) 64
    (C) 24
    (D) 16

14. $\Delta + \square = 10$

   $\square - \Delta = 2$

   The two sentences shown above are true. Which of the following values for Δ and $\square$ make both number sentences true?

   (A) 4, 6   (B) 8, 2

   (C) 7, 3   (D) 8, 6

15. The sum of the numbers shown by two abacuses is ___________.

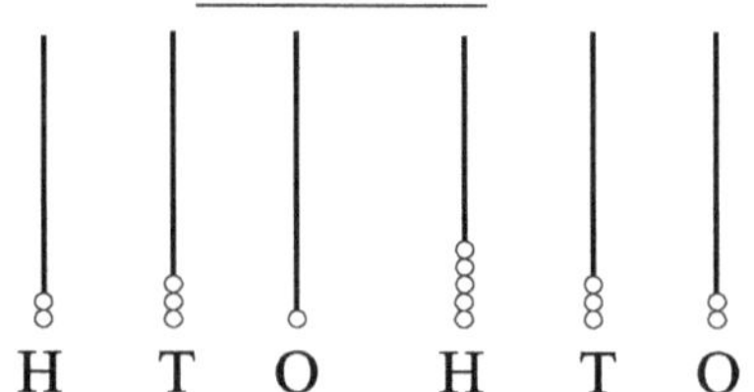

   (A) 750   (B) 663

   (C) 763   (D) 762

16. After spending ₹ 260, Hari had left ₹ 300. left. How did he have at first?

   (A) ₹ 300   (B) ₹ 560

   (C) ₹ 40   (D) ₹ 260

17. Rita collected 630 stamps. She gave 50 stamps to Ram. How many stamps had Rita left?

   (A) 580   (B) 680

   (C) 620   (D) 130

18. Bunny puts 235 jelly beans in a bottle. He needs 80 more jelly beans to fill up the bottle. How many jelly beans can the bottle hold?

   (A) 195

   (B) 395

   (C) 155

   (D) 315

19. Amit bought 2 items from his school bookshop. The items cost ₹ 50 in all. Which 2 items did he buy?.

Toy car	₹ 35
Story book	₹ 25
Pencil box	₹ 15
Water bottle	₹ 20

   (A) A pencil box and story book

   (B) A toy car and a story book

   (C) 2 water bottles

   (D) 2 story books

20. There are 300 students in a school. If 125 of them are girls, then find the number of boys.

   (A) 275

   (B) 175

   (C) 225

   (D) 169

HOTS (ACHIEVERS SECTION)

21. Find the values of x, y and z.

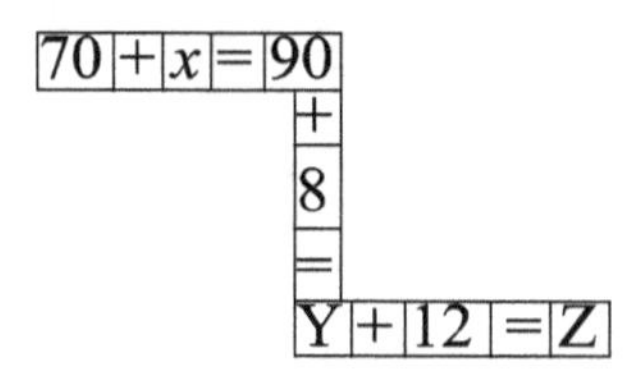

   (A) 20, 98, 110   (B) 30, 100, 120

   (C) 15, 95, 115   (D) 10, 90, 110

22. Shradha had ₹ 300. Her father gave her ₹ 550 as pocket money. She got ₹ 1000 from a price distribution in her school. How much money Shradha has now?

   (A) ₹ 1300   (B) ₹ 850

   (C) ₹ 1850   (D) ₹ 1550

23. Find P.

$$\begin{array}{r} 8\ P \\ -5\ \ 4 \\ \hline 2\ \ 9 \end{array}$$

   (A) 4   (B) 3

   (C) 8   (D) 2

24. What must be subtracted from 956 to get 500?
   (A) 200 (B) 256
   (C) 456 (D) 500

25. Subtract the sum of 55 and 45 from the sum of 60 and 70.
   (A) 20 (B) 15
   (C) 5 (D) 30

1.	A B C D	6.	A B C D	11.	A B C D	16	A B C D	21.	A B C D
2.	A B C D	7.	A B C D	12.	A B C D	17.	A B C D	22.	A B C D
3.	A B C D	8.	A B C D	13.	A B C D	18.	A B C D	23.	A B C D
4.	A B C D	9.	A B C D	14.	A B C D	19.	A B C D	24.	A B C D
5.	A B C D	10.	A B C D	15.	A B C D	20.	A B C D	25.	A B C D

MULTIPLICATION AND DIVISION

LEARNING OBJECTIVES

➤ Properties of Multiplication
➤ Multiplying by Tens and Hundreds

➤ Properties of Division
➤ Multiplication and Division Facts

MULTIPLE CHOICE QUESTIONS

1. Find the value of A.

$$
\begin{array}{r}
A\ 3 \\
\times\ 5 \\
\hline
2\ 1\ 5 \\
\hline
\end{array}
$$

  (A) 1   (B) 2
  (C) 3   (D) 4

2. Find the missing number.

16, 20, 24, 28, ? 36, 40

  (A) 30   (B) 32
  (C) 34   (D) 38

3. 3×4 is _____ more than 2×4.

  (A) 2   (B) 3
  (C) 6   (D) 4

4. 9×5 is _____ more than 8×5.

  (A) 9   (B) 8
  (C) 5   (D) 1

5. $2 \times 10 = 4 \times$ _____

  (A) 5   (B) 8
  (C) 10   (D) 4

6. _____ $\times 10 = 5 \times 6$

  (A) 30   (B) 3
  (C) 5   (D) 60

7. There are 2 buttons in each t-shirt. How many buttons are there in 6 t-shirts?

  (A) 2   (B) 6
  (C) 24   (D) 12

8. There are 4 flowers in each pot. How many flowers are there in 5 pots?

  (A) 4   (B) 5
  (C) 20   (D) 10

9. Each chair has 4 legs. How many legs do 5 chairs have?

  (A) 4   (B) 5
  (C) 10   (D) 20

10. An ant has 6 legs. How many pairs of legs do 7 ants have?

   1 pair of legs = 2 legs
(A) 21
(B) 42
(C) 7
(D) None of these

11. $(27 \div 3) \times 8 =$ _______
(A) 24   (B) 27
(C) 42   (D) 72

12. If we start subtracting 4 from 19 stepwise as shown, we will be able to subtract 4 times.
$$19 - 4 = 15$$
$$15 - 4 = 11$$
$$11 - 4 = 7$$
$$7 - 4 = 3$$

If we start subtracting 4 from 84 in a similar manner, how many times will we be able to subtract?
(A) 21   (B) 42
(C) 68   (D) 84

13. If this pattern continues, then what is the next number?

80, 40, 20, _______

14. 3 tens $\div$ 3 = _______
(A) 1   (B) 10
(C) 90   (D) 100

15. How many threes are there in the sum of 63 and 27.
(A) 3   (B) 9
(C) 21   (D) 30

16. _______ $\div 3 = 5 \times 5$
(A) 15   (B) 75
(C) 90   (D) 60

17. If $5 \times 3 = 15$ then $15 \div 3 =$ _______
(A) 15   (B) 3
(C) 5   (D) 4

18. If $6 \times 4 =$ _______ then _______ $\div 4 =$ _______
(A) 24, 24, 6
(B) 24, 6, 24
(C) 24, 4, 24
(D) 24, , 24, 4

19. $20 \div 1 =$ _______
(A) 1   (B) 20
(C) 0   (D) 2

20. _______ $\div 7 = 0$
(A) 1   (B) 0
(C) 7   (D) 14

HOTS (ACHIEVERS SECTION)

21. The number of legs of 8 rabbits is _______.
(A) 16 tens + 5 ones
(B) 32 ones
(C) 3 tens − 2 tens
(D) 2 tens − 4 ones

22. Apples are sold at ₹100 per kg. Jasmine has ₹1000. If she bought 5 kg of apples, how much money is left with her now?
(A) 500   (B) 400
(C) 600   (D) 100

23. Find the dividend if:

Divisor   = 16
Quotient   = 7
Remainder   = 2
(A) 110   (B) 112
(C) 114   (D) 120

24. $0 \div (2{\times}4+5{\times}5) =$ __________ .

    (A) 5   (B) 10

    (C) 15   (D) 0

25. Divide the sum of 92 and 52 by the sum of 9 and 7?

    (A) 9   (B) 8

    (C) 10   (D) 12

1.	Ⓐ Ⓑ Ⓒ Ⓓ	6.	Ⓐ Ⓑ Ⓒ Ⓓ	11.	Ⓐ Ⓑ Ⓒ Ⓓ	16	Ⓐ Ⓑ Ⓒ Ⓓ	21.	Ⓐ Ⓑ Ⓒ Ⓓ
2.	Ⓐ Ⓑ Ⓒ Ⓓ	7.	Ⓐ Ⓑ Ⓒ Ⓓ	12.	Ⓐ Ⓑ Ⓒ Ⓓ	17.	Ⓐ Ⓑ Ⓒ Ⓓ	22.	Ⓐ Ⓑ Ⓒ Ⓓ
3.	Ⓐ Ⓑ Ⓒ Ⓓ	8.	Ⓐ Ⓑ Ⓒ Ⓓ	13.	Ⓐ Ⓑ Ⓒ Ⓓ	18.	Ⓐ Ⓑ Ⓒ Ⓓ	23.	Ⓐ Ⓑ Ⓒ Ⓓ
4.	Ⓐ Ⓑ Ⓒ Ⓓ	9.	Ⓐ Ⓑ Ⓒ Ⓓ	14.	Ⓐ Ⓑ Ⓒ Ⓓ	19.	Ⓐ Ⓑ Ⓒ Ⓓ	24.	Ⓐ Ⓑ Ⓒ Ⓓ
5.	Ⓐ Ⓑ Ⓒ Ⓓ	10.	Ⓐ Ⓑ Ⓒ Ⓓ	15.	Ⓐ Ⓑ Ⓒ Ⓓ	20.	Ⓐ Ⓑ Ⓒ Ⓓ	25.	Ⓐ Ⓑ Ⓒ Ⓓ

MULTIPLICATION AND DIVISION

LEARNING OBJECTIVES

➤ Properties of Division

➤ Multiplication and Division Facts

➤ Tests of Division

MULTIPLE CHOICE QUESTIONS

Direction (1–5) : Study the given figure and answer the following questions :

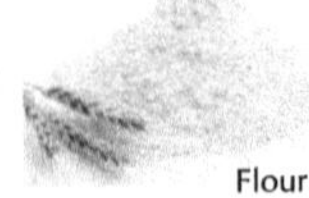
Flour
350 gm

Coffee Powder
150 gm

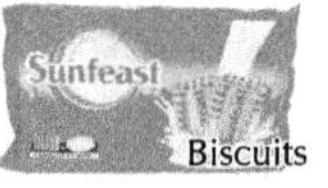
Biscuits
200 gm

1. The weight of the packet of biscuits is- _______ g lighter than the weight of the packet of flour.
   (A) 300   (B) 200
   (C) 150   (D) 250

2. The weight of 2 packets of flour is _______ g.
   (A) 800   (B) 750
   (C) 500   (D) 700

3. The weight of 4 packets of biscuits is _______ g.
   (A) 800   (B) 300
   (C) 650   (D) 700

4. The weight of 1 bag of flour is _______ g less than 4 packets of biscuits.
   (A) 250   (B) 350
   (C) 450   (D) 300

5. The total weight of 1 bag of flour, 1 packet of coffee powder and 1 packet of biscuit is _______ g.
   (A) 400   (B) 300
   (C) 700   (D) 500

Direction (6–10) : Water in each of the following containers is poured into cups. Study the picture and answer the following questions :

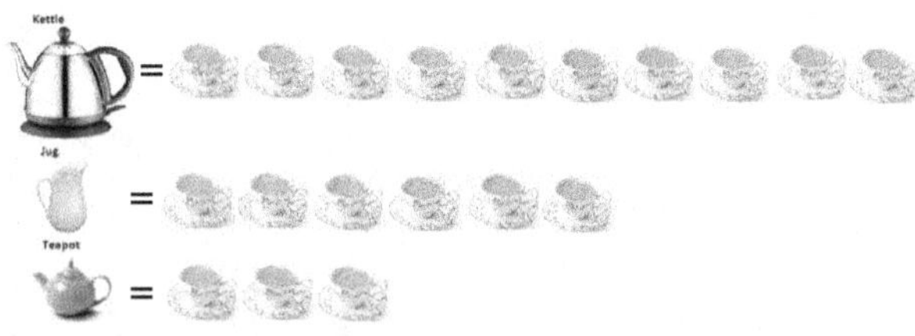

6. _______ cups of tea can fill 3 teapots.
   (A) 6   (B) 8
   (C) 9   (D) 7

7. The _______ has the least amount of tea.
   (A) Kettle   (B) Teapot
   (C) Jug   (D) Kettle and jug

8. The _______ has the most amount of tea.
   (A) Jug
   (B) Teapot
   (C) Kettle
   (D) Kettle and jug

9. The _______ holds 5 fewer cups of tea than the kettle.
   (A) Jug   (B) Teapot
   (C) Can't say   (D) None of these

10. The total volume of teapot and the jug is _______ more cup of the tea than the kettle.
    (A) 2   (B) 3
    (C) 4   (D) 1

11. What is the weight of the pineapple?

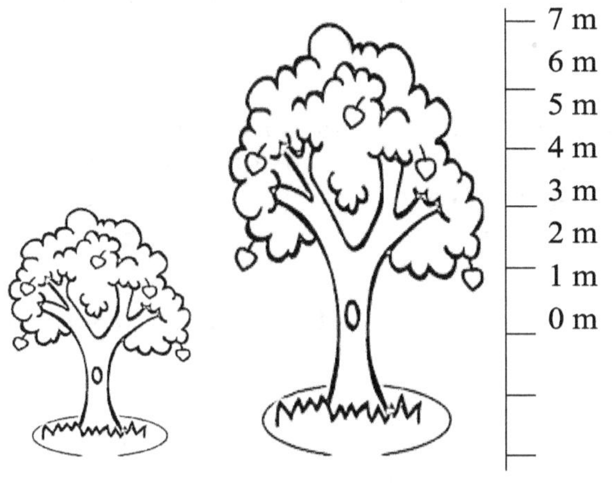

    (A) 500g   (B) 1Kg
    (C) 1 kg 50g   (D) 100g

12. What is the difference between heights of both the trees?

    (A) 2 m   (B) 3 m
    (C) 4 m   (D) 5 m

13. Which block is heaviest among all four?
    (A) 150 Kg   (B) 1 Kg 50 g
    (C) 1.50 Kg   (D) 15000g

14. If ⊔ + ⊔ + ⊔ = 3 Litres, then ⊔ = _______
    (A) 2 Litres   (B) 1 Litre
    (C) 3 Litres   (D) None of these

15. How much more weight should be put to balance the weighing machine?

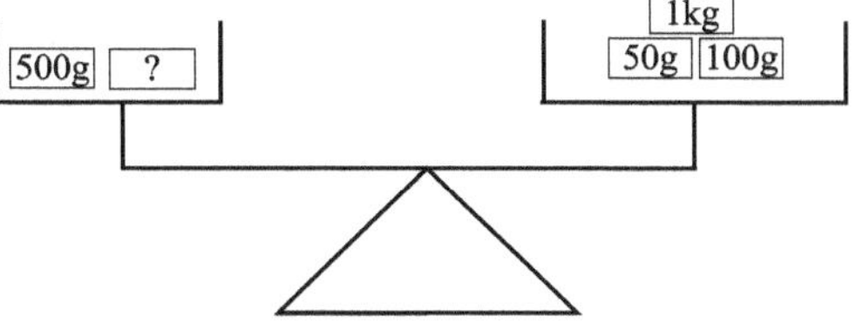

    (A) 400 g   (B) 650 Kg
    (C) 650 g   (D) 600 g

16. The distance between Veeru's home and his school is 456 m. After walking 187m. from his home, Veeru realized that he forgot it bring his pencil box. He walked back home to get it and then walked to school. What is the total distance travelled by him?
    (A) 269 + 187   (D) 456 + 187
    (C) 456 + 187 + 187   (D) 266 + 187

17. Seema is taking part in a race. She has to run for 500 m, swim for 350 m, and then cycle for another 150 m. After one hour, she still have 45 m more to complete. What distance travelled by Seema in one hour?
    (A) 1045 m   (B) 955 m
    (C) 1000 m   (D) 910 m

18. A snail fell into a well. The well is 30 m tall. Every day, it can climb 6 m but will sip 2 m down. How many days will take to reach the top?
    (A) 8   (B) 7
    (C) 6   (D) 5

19. A packet of milk is 432 g heavier than a packet of orange juice . The weight of the packet of orange juice is 212 g. What is the total mass of the packet of milk and orange juice?
    (A) 950   (B) 856
    (C) 986   (D) 748

20. Amit's weight is 50 kg. He is 4 kg heavier than Meena. Balaji is 5 kg heavier than Amit. Total weight of all is _______ kg.
    (A) 165   (B) 160
    (C) 151   (D) 132

21. It takes 12 glasses of water to fill up the jug. It takes 3 bowls to fill a glass. How many bowls of water will be required to fill the jug?

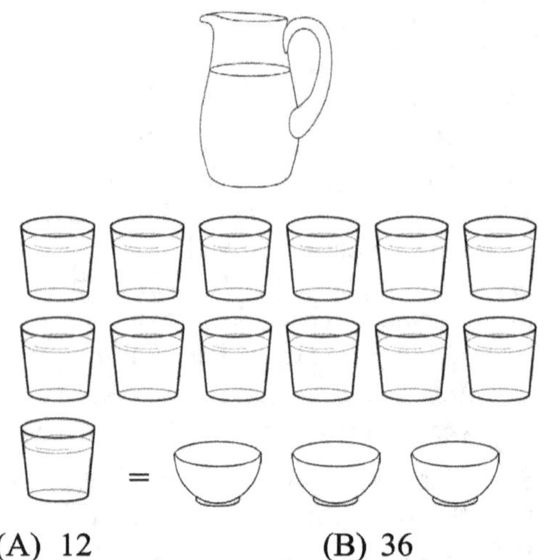

(A) 12
(B) 36
(C) 24
(D) None of these

Directions : Look at the diagram below and answer the given questions :

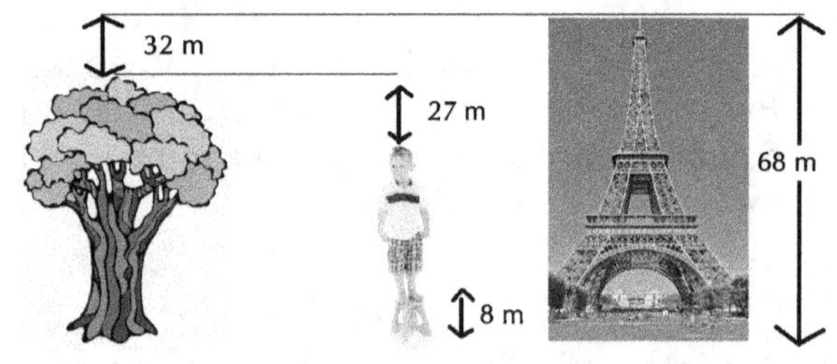

22. The tree is __________ m tall.
(A) 36
(B) 34
(C) 28
(D) 32

23. Sita weighs 40 kg. Kavita weighs 4 kg less than Sita. Rina weighs 6 kg more than Kavita. What is the weight of Kavita?
(A) 30 kg
(B) 36 kg
(C) 42 kg
(D) 40 kg

Direction (24–25)

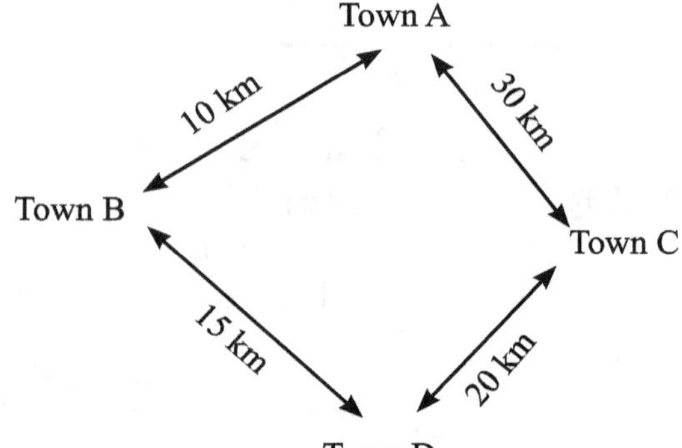

24. What is the total distance that Kavya needs to cover to go to town B from A by crossing town C and town D?
(A) 30 km
(B) 10 km
(C) 65 km
(D) 70 km

25. What is the shortest distance from town A to town B?
(A) 30 km
(B) 10 km
(C) 65 km
(D) 70 km

—Darken Your Choice with HB Pencil—

1.	A B C D	6.	A B C D	11.	A B C D	16	A B C D	21.	A B C D
2.	A B C D	7.	A B C D	12.	A B C D	17.	A B C D	22.	A B C D
3.	A B C D	8.	A B C D	13.	A B C D	18.	A B C D	23.	A B C D
4.	A B C D	9.	A B C D	14.	A B C D	19.	A B C D	24.	A B C D
5.	A B C D	10.	A B C D	15.	A B C D	20.	A B C D	25.	A B C D

TIME AND MONEY

LEARNING OBJECTIVES

➤ Time
➤ Calendar

➤ Money
➤ Important Points about Money

MULTIPLE CHOICE QUESTIONS

1. How many months in a year have 31 days?
   (A) 8
   (B) 7
   (C) 6
   (d) 5

2. How many times does long hand of a clock take to complete its three rounds?
   (A) 2 hours
   (B) 2 hours 30 minutes
   (C) 60 minutes
   (d) 3 hours

3. The month with neither 31 days nor 30 days is ______
   (A) February
   (B) April
   (C) November
   (d) December

4. 135 hours = ______
   (A) 5 days
   (B) 5 days 10 hours
   (C) 5 days 15 hours
   (d) None of these

5. How many months in a year have 30 days?
   (A) 6
   (B) 5
   (C) 4
   (d) None of these

6. The hour hand takes ______ hours to move from 2 to 5.
   (A) 3
   (B) 1
   (C) 2
   (d) 6

7. 105 hours = ______
   (a) 4 days
   (b) 4 days 9 hours
   (c) 4 days 15 hours
   (d) None of these

8. The month with 31 days is ______.
   (A) February
   (B) April
   (C) November
   (d) December

9. The month with 30 days is/are ______.
   (A) April
   (B) November
   (C) June
   (d) All of these

10. When the short hand is at 2 and the long hand is at 12, the time is ______.
    (A) 2 O'clock
    (B) 12 O'clock
    (C) 14 O'clock
    (d) None of these

11. If Shraddha buys a handbag and another item, she will have ₹ 11 left. Other item she buys is ______.
    (A) Lipstick
    (B) Dress
    (C) A pair of shoes
    (d) Mirror

12. After Shraddha bought two of the items, she has ₹ 63 left. What items did she buy?
   (A) Dress, mirror
   (B) Lipstick, mirror
   (C) A pair of shoes ,lipstick
   (D) Dress, comb

Direction (8–14) : Study the table below carefully and answer the following questions:

Item	Price
Eraser	25 paise
Correction pen	₹1
Ruler	50 paise
Exercise book	65 paise
Pen	₹2
Text book	₹4

13. Parveen wants to buy 2 erasers and 1 ruler. He needs _______ altogether.
   (A) 50 paise
   (B) 75 paise
   (C) ₹ 1
   (D) None of these

14. Kuku spent ₹ 10 to buy 2 textbook and a _______.
   (A) Correction pen
   (B) Eraser
   (C) Ruler
   (D) Pen

15. Anita bought 2 pens, 3 correction pens and a text book. She spend ₹ _______ altogether.
   (A) 11 (B) 9
   (C) 13 (D) 10

16. Vinay bought a textbook and he gave the cashier ₹ 10. He received ₹ _____ change.
   (A) 8 (B) 6
   (C) 4 (D) 2

17. Viru wants to buy an exercise book but he only has 45 paise. He will need _______ more.
   (A) 25 paise (B) 15 paise
   (C) 20 paise (D) 30 paise

18. Harish spent ₹ 10. He bought twice as many correction pens as rulers. He bought _______ correction pens and _______ ruler.
   (A) 6, 2 (B) 6, 4
   (C) 8, 2 (D) 8, 4

19. Mohit spent ₹ 10 to buy correction pens and rulers. He bought 4 more rulers than Harish. He bought _______ correction pens and _______ rulers.
   (A) 6, 8 (B) 6, 4
   (C) 4, 6 (D) 8, 4

20. The sum of five ₹ 10 notes and five ₹ 20 notes is _______.
   (A) ₹ 100 (B) ₹ 150
   (C) ₹ 50 (D) ₹ 200

HOTS (ACHIEVERS SECTION)

21. Sheetal started walking to temple at 5:25 p.m. She reached the temple at 5.50 p.m. How long did she take to walk to the temple?
   (A) 20 mins (B) 25 mins
   (C) 30 mins (D) 35 mins

22. Ankit starts his guitar parctice from 1st November 20XX. He practices for 10 days and then takes 2 days break. Again he practices for 2 days, his practice finishes on _______.

November 20XX

Mon	Tue	Wed	Thu	Fri	Sat	Sun
				1	2	3
4	5	6	7	8	9	10
11	12	13	14	15	16	17
18	19	20	21	22	23	24
25	26	27	28	29	30	

   (A) 13th November (B) 15th November
   (C) 14th November (D) 16th November

23. Preeti has ₹ 500. If she bought 25 oranges each for ₹ 9. Which expression shows the correct amount of change that she will get back?

(A) 500 + 25

(B) 500 + 25 × 9

(C) 500 − 25 × 9

(D) 500 × 25 + 9

24. Ricky opened up his piggy bank to buy a robot of Rs. 200. In her piggy bank she found 10 coins of Rs. 10, 9 coins ₹ 5 and 5 coins of ₹ 2. How much more money does she need to buy robot?

(A) ₹ 50

(B) ₹ 60

(C) ₹ 40

(D) ₹ 45

25. A family went to a mall. They spent Rs. 70 on ice-cream, Rs. 85 on balloons and Rs. 155 for tickets of a drama. How much did the family spend at the mall?

(A) ₹ 310

(B) ₹ 300

(C) ₹ 350

(D) ₹ 410

Darken Your Choice with HB Pencil

1.	Ⓐ Ⓑ Ⓒ Ⓓ	6.	Ⓐ Ⓑ Ⓒ Ⓓ	11.	Ⓐ Ⓑ Ⓒ Ⓓ	16	Ⓐ Ⓑ Ⓒ Ⓓ	21.	Ⓐ Ⓑ Ⓒ Ⓓ
2.	Ⓐ Ⓑ Ⓒ Ⓓ	7.	Ⓐ Ⓑ Ⓒ Ⓓ	12.	Ⓐ Ⓑ Ⓒ Ⓓ	17.	Ⓐ Ⓑ Ⓒ Ⓓ	22.	Ⓐ Ⓑ Ⓒ Ⓓ
3.	Ⓐ Ⓑ Ⓒ Ⓓ	8.	Ⓐ Ⓑ Ⓒ Ⓓ	13.	Ⓐ Ⓑ Ⓒ Ⓓ	18.	Ⓐ Ⓑ Ⓒ Ⓓ	23.	Ⓐ Ⓑ Ⓒ Ⓓ
4.	Ⓐ Ⓑ Ⓒ Ⓓ	9.	Ⓐ Ⓑ Ⓒ Ⓓ	14.	Ⓐ Ⓑ Ⓒ Ⓓ	19.	Ⓐ Ⓑ Ⓒ Ⓓ	24.	Ⓐ Ⓑ Ⓒ Ⓓ
5.	Ⓐ Ⓑ Ⓒ Ⓓ	10.	Ⓐ Ⓑ Ⓒ Ⓓ	15.	Ⓐ Ⓑ Ⓒ Ⓓ	20.	Ⓐ Ⓑ Ⓒ Ⓓ	25.	Ⓐ Ⓑ Ⓒ Ⓓ

GEOMETRICAL SHAPES

LEARNING OBJECTIVES

- ➤ Point and Line
- ➤ Types of Line
- ➤ Plane Shapes
- ➤ Solid Shapes

MULTIPLE CHOICE QUESTIONS

1. Given line is _________ .

  (A) Curved   (B) Slant
  (C) Straight   (D) None of these

2. Count the vertical lines in the given figure.

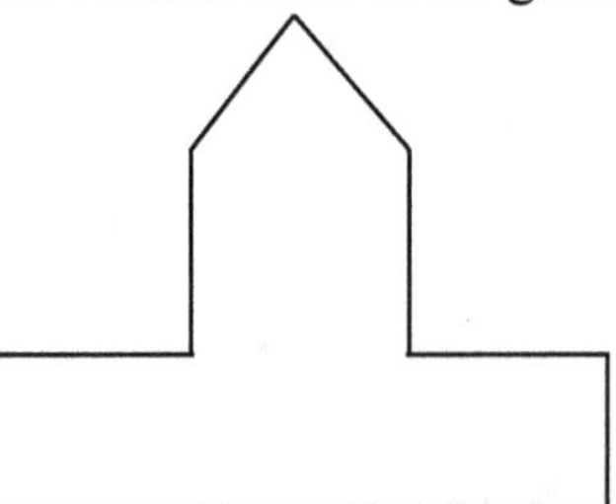

  (A) 1   (B) 2
  (C) 3   (D) 4

3. The line | is _______ .

  (A) Slant   (B) Curved
  (C) Vertical   (D) None of these

4. The line / is ______ .

  (A) Slant
  (B) Curved
  (C) Straight
  (D) None of these

Direction (5–6) : See the given figure and and answer the questions

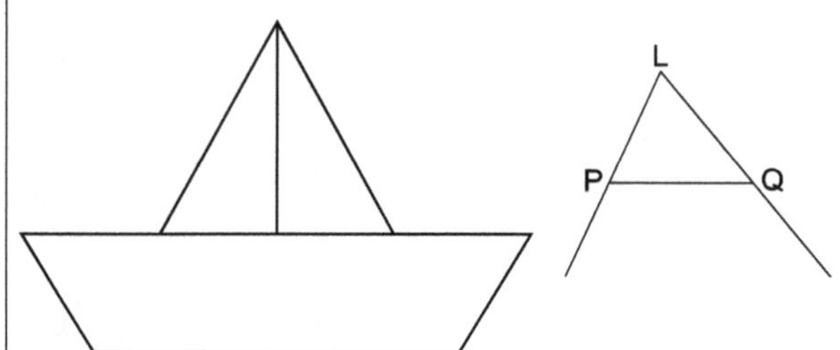

5. Count the slanting lines in the figure.

  (A) 4   (B) 3
  (C) 6   (D) 5

6. Count the total lines in the figure.

  (A) 6   (B) 7
  (C) 5   (D) 8

7. A rectangle has _______ sides.

  (A) 2   (B) 4
  (C) 6   (D) 0

8. A square has _______ corners.

  (A) 4   (B) 6
  (C) 2   (D) 0

9. A rectangle has _______ corners.

(A) 4   (B) 6

(C) 2   (D) 0

10. An oval has _______ sides.

(A) 0   (B) 1

(C) 2   (D) 3

11. A cube has _______ flat faces.

(A) 6   (B) 4

(C) 2   (D) 8

12. A cone has _______ curved face.

(A) 1   (B) 2

(C) 3   (D) 4

13. Flat face of a cube is a _______ .

(A) Square   (B) Rectangle

(C) Oval   (D) Triangle

14. Match the shaded face of objects with the correct shape.

A.		1.	
B.		2.	
C.		3.	
D.		4.	

Codes

	A	B	C	D
(A)	1	2	3	4
(B)	3	4	2	1
(C)	2	1	3	4
(D)	3	4	1	2

15. What is the shape of base of a cylinder?

(A) Circle   (B) Square

(C) Rectangle   (D) None of these

16. Naina has 5 matchsticks. She made a design with these matchsticks. Which of the following is the possible design made by her, if her design has two slanting, two standing and one sleeping line?

(A)   (A)

(C)   (D) None of these

17. Rohan wants to make a cube shaped box. How many squares he needs to make the box?

(A) 5   (B) 6

(C) 7   (D) 4

18. Santa has to make a model of a rocket. Which two shapes he needs two make the following model?

(A) Cone and cube   (B) Sphere and cone

(C) Cone and cylinder   (D) None of these

19. Sohan has some erasers.

These are _______ lines in the erasers altogether.

(A) 31   (B) 29

(C) 30   (D) 32

20. If Neha places some rectangles above the other, then which shape she will get?

(A) Cone   (B) Sphere

(C) Cube   (D) Cuboid

21. Shape __________ has largest number of sides.

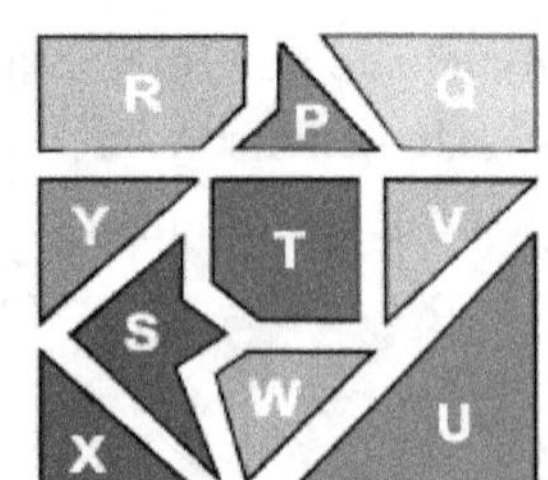

(A) T
(B) R
(C) S
(D) P

22. Look at the given shapes.

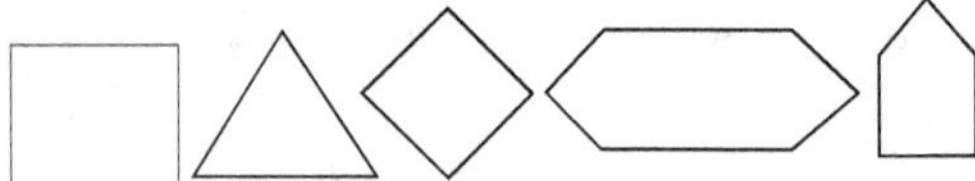

Which statement is correct?

(i) All the shapes are made up of straight lines.

(ii) All the shapes have up exactly four lines.

(iii) All the shapes are made of curved lines.

(A) (i)
(B) (ii)
(C) (iii)
(D) Both (i) and (ii)

23. How many 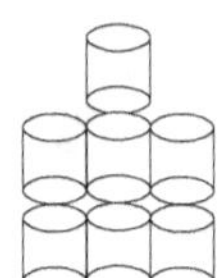 are there in given figures?

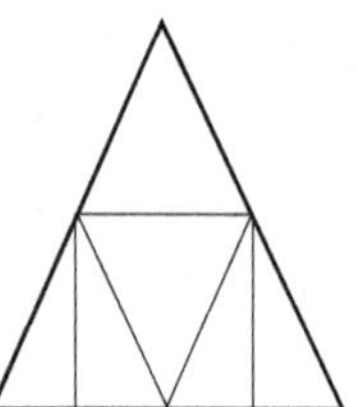

(A) 7
(B) 12
(C) 10
(D) None of these

24. Count the triangles.

(A) 5
(B) 10
(C) 9
(D) 12

25. Identify the figure.

I have two circular faces and one curved face. I have no corners. Soft drink cans often look like me. Who am I?

(A) Cuboid
(B) Cylinder
(C) Cone
(D) Cube

Darken Your Choice with HB Pencil

	A B C D		A B C D		A B C D		A B C D		A B C D
1.	Ⓐ Ⓑ Ⓒ Ⓓ	6.	Ⓐ Ⓑ Ⓒ Ⓓ	11.	Ⓐ Ⓑ Ⓒ Ⓓ	16	Ⓐ Ⓑ Ⓒ Ⓓ	21.	Ⓐ Ⓑ Ⓒ Ⓓ
2.	Ⓐ Ⓑ Ⓒ Ⓓ	7.	Ⓐ Ⓑ Ⓒ Ⓓ	12.	Ⓐ Ⓑ Ⓒ Ⓓ	17.	Ⓐ Ⓑ Ⓒ Ⓓ	22.	Ⓐ Ⓑ Ⓒ Ⓓ
3.	Ⓐ Ⓑ Ⓒ Ⓓ	8.	Ⓐ Ⓑ Ⓒ Ⓓ	13.	Ⓐ Ⓑ Ⓒ Ⓓ	18.	Ⓐ Ⓑ Ⓒ Ⓓ	23.	Ⓐ Ⓑ Ⓒ Ⓓ
4.	Ⓐ Ⓑ Ⓒ Ⓓ	9.	Ⓐ Ⓑ Ⓒ Ⓓ	14.	Ⓐ Ⓑ Ⓒ Ⓓ	19.	Ⓐ Ⓑ Ⓒ Ⓓ	24.	Ⓐ Ⓑ Ⓒ Ⓓ
5.	Ⓐ Ⓑ Ⓒ Ⓓ	10.	Ⓐ Ⓑ Ⓒ Ⓓ	15.	Ⓐ Ⓑ Ⓒ Ⓓ	20.	Ⓐ Ⓑ Ⓒ Ⓓ	25.	Ⓐ Ⓑ Ⓒ Ⓓ

PATTERNS

LEARNING OBJECTIVES

➤ Concept of Pattern

MULTIPLE CHOICE QUESTIONS

1. What are the next two shapes to complete the pattern?

   (A) Circle, circle
   (B) Triangle, circle
   (C) Circle, triangle
   (D) Square, circle

2. What are the next two shapes to complete the pattern?

   (A) Circle, circle
   (B) Triangle, square
   (C) Circle, triangle
   (D) Square, circle

3. Find the number pattern in star A. The first point has a value of 3. Then look at star B. Use the same number pattern to figure out the value of the other points.

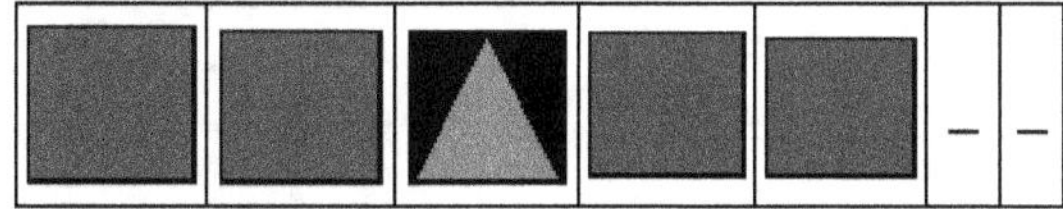

   (A) 5, 7, 9, 18
   (B) 4, 6, 8, 10

   (C) 6, 10, 14, 18
   (D) 10, 12, 14, 16

4. What number should be on the other points of star B if you follow the same pattern?

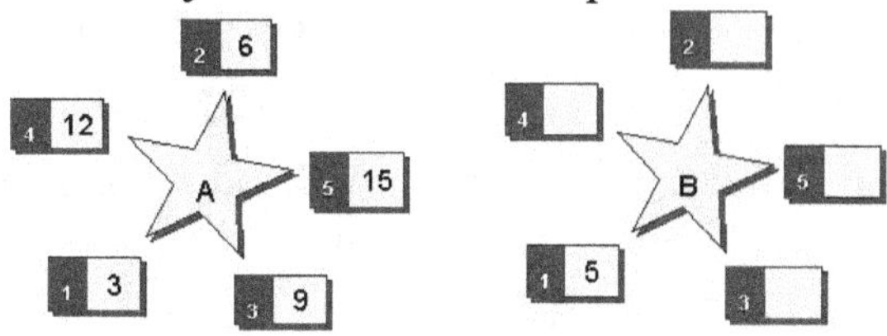

   (A) 5, 7, 9, 18
   (B) 8, 11, 15, 17
   (C) 6, 10, 14, 18
   (D) 10, 15, 20, 25

5. Write the next 3 numbers in the pattern.
   30, 32, 34, ___, ___, ___
   (A) 36, 38, 40   (B) 34, 36, 38
   (C) 36, 40, 44   (D) None of these

6. Write the next 3 numbers in the pattern.
   5, 10, 15, ___, ___, ___
   (A) 25, 30, 35   (B) 20, 25, 30
   (C) 25, 35, 45   (D) 20, 30, 40

7. Write the next 3 numbers in the pattern.
   27, 24, 21, ___, ___, ___
   (A) 15, 12, 10   (B) 20, 19, 18
   (C) 18, 15, 12   (D) None of these

8. Write the next 3 numbers in the pattern.

24, 20, 16, ___, ___, ___

(A) 10, 8, 6   (B) 4, 6, 8

(C) 6, 10, 14   (D) 12, 8, 4

9. Write the numbers to complete the table given below.

IN	2	3	4	5	8	10
OUT	4	5	6			

(A) 7, 10, 12   (B) 4, 6, 8

(C) 6, 10, 14   (D) 12, 8, 4

10. Write the numbers to complete the table given below.

IN	4	5	6	7	9	10
OUT	8	9	10			

(A) 10, 8, 6   (B) 11, 13, 14

(C) 6, 10, 14   (D) 12, 8, 4

11. Find the letter which will end the first word and start the second word.

      MA?ET

(A) K   (B) T

(C) N   (D) L

12. Find the rule followed in the figure pattern and missing figure.

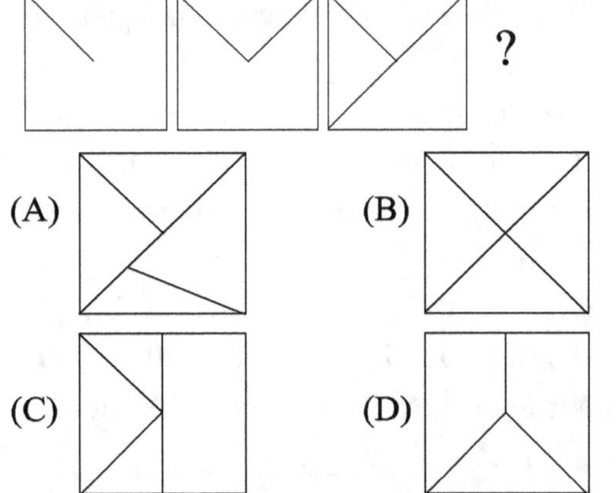

13. Which of the following replaces the question mark (?) so that figure series is formed?

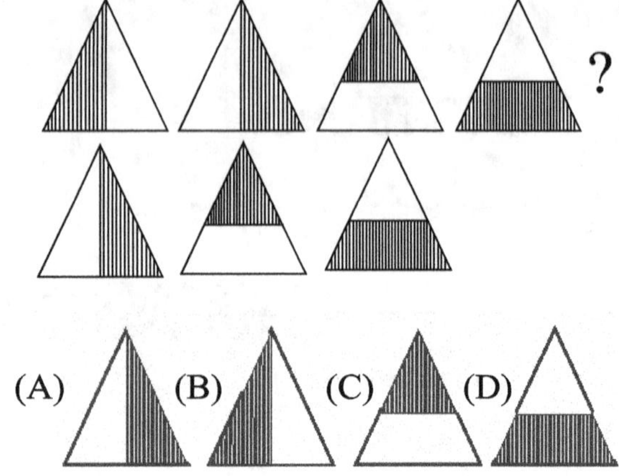

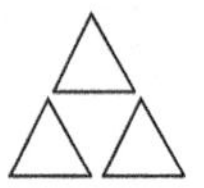 (A) 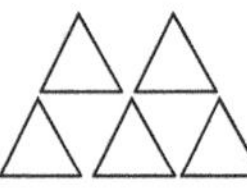 (B) (C) (D) 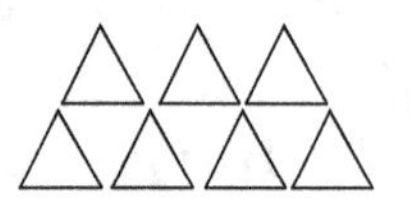

14. Which is the next letter?

D B A C D B A C D B A C D B - -

(A) DB   (B) CD

(C) AC   (D) BA

15. How many triangles will be there in pattern 4?

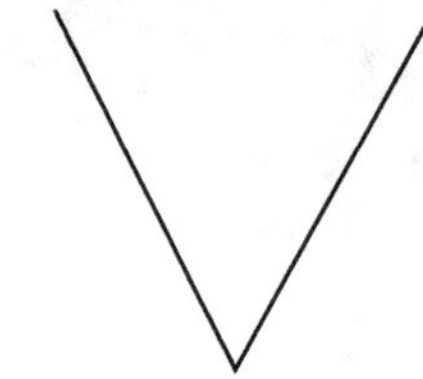

Pattern 1   Pattern 2   Pattern3

(A) 9   (B) 10

(C) 11   (D) 12

16. In which of the following figure, Shape (X) is exactly embedded?

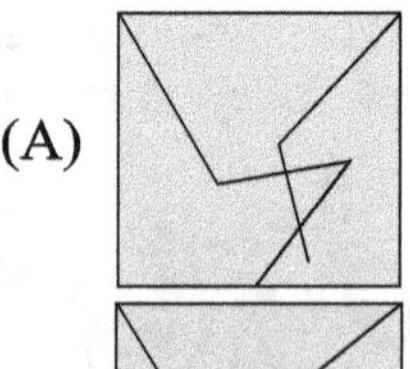

Shape (X)

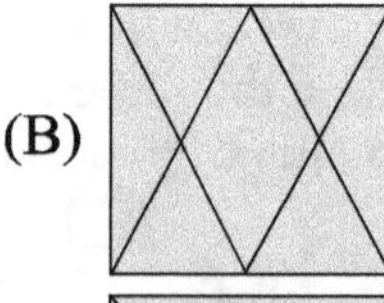 (A)   (B)

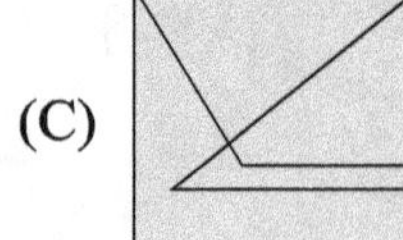 (C)   (D) 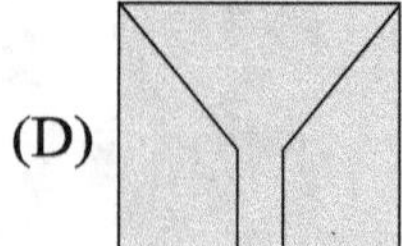

17. Find P and Q respectively.

○	△	□
△	□	P
□	Q	△

(A) △□ (B) □□

(C) △△ (D) ○○

18. Find the missing clock if given pattern is followed on the clocks.

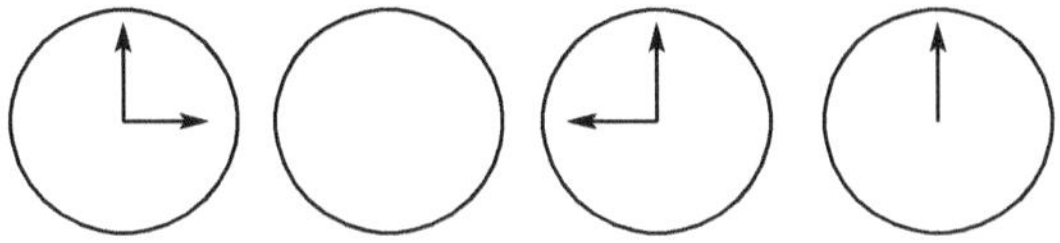

(A) 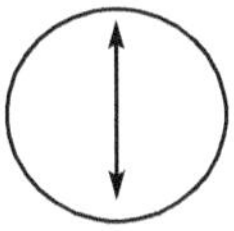 (B) 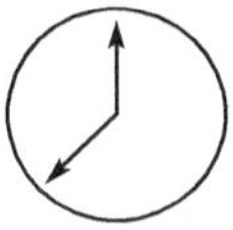

(C) 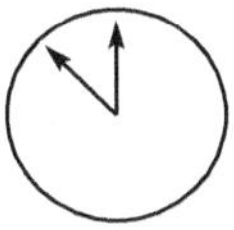 (D) 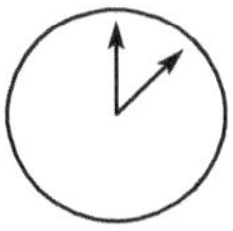

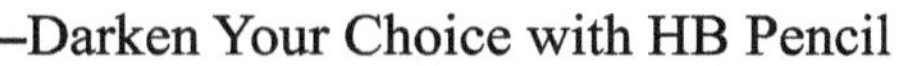

19. Which of the following figures will complete the pattern in figure (x)?

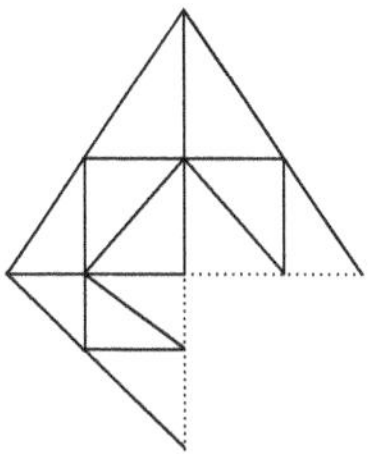

figure (x)

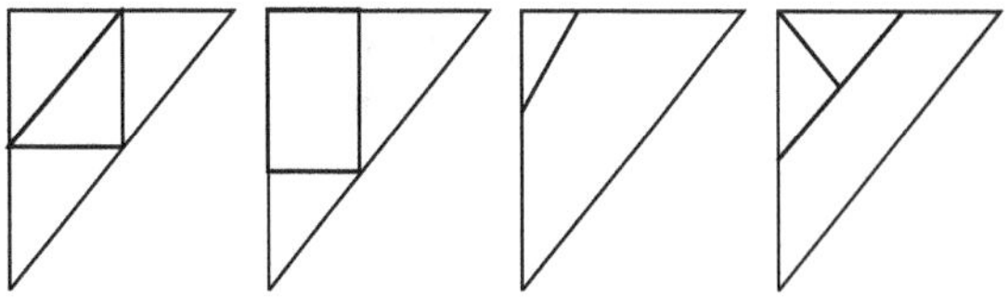

(A) (B) (C) (D)

20. How many pencils will be there in pattern 4 ?

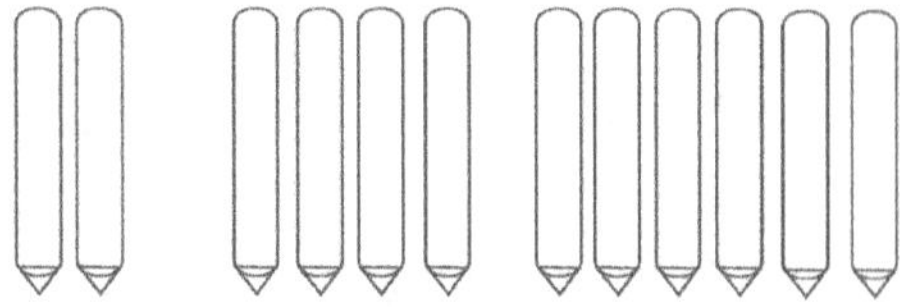

Pattern 1 Pattern 2 Pattern 3

(A) 14 (B) 12

(C) 8 (D) 16

Darken Your Choice with HB Pencil

1. Ⓐ Ⓑ Ⓒ Ⓓ	5. Ⓐ Ⓑ Ⓒ Ⓓ	9. Ⓐ Ⓑ Ⓒ Ⓓ	13. Ⓐ Ⓑ Ⓒ Ⓓ	17. Ⓐ Ⓑ Ⓒ Ⓓ
2. Ⓐ Ⓑ Ⓒ Ⓓ	6. Ⓐ Ⓑ Ⓒ Ⓓ	10. Ⓐ Ⓑ Ⓒ Ⓓ	14. Ⓐ Ⓑ Ⓒ Ⓓ	18. Ⓐ Ⓑ Ⓒ Ⓓ
3. Ⓐ Ⓑ Ⓒ Ⓓ	7. Ⓐ Ⓑ Ⓒ Ⓓ	11. Ⓐ Ⓑ Ⓒ Ⓓ	15. Ⓐ Ⓑ Ⓒ Ⓓ	19. Ⓐ Ⓑ Ⓒ Ⓓ
4. Ⓐ Ⓑ Ⓒ Ⓓ	8. Ⓐ Ⓑ Ⓒ Ⓓ	12. Ⓐ Ⓑ Ⓒ Ⓓ	16. Ⓐ Ⓑ Ⓒ Ⓓ	20. Ⓐ Ⓑ Ⓒ Ⓓ

PICTOGRAPHS

LEARNING OBJECTIVES

➤ Pictographs

MULTIPLE CHOICE QUESTIONS

Direction (1–4) : The picture graph below shows the number of cookies 5 children ate. Study the graph and answer the given questions.

Number of cookies each child ate	
Ram	🍪🍪🍪🍪🍪
Aman	🍪🍪
Sumit	🍪🍪🍪
Karan	🍪🍪🍪🍪
Aayush	🍪🍪🍪🍪🍪🍪🍪

Each 🍪 stands for 3

1. ________________ ate the most number of cookies.
   - (A) Aayush
   - (B) Ram
   - (C) Karan
   - (D) Sumit

2. Sumit ate __________ cookies.
   - (A) 3
   - (B) 6
   - (C) 9
   - (D) 12

3. ______ and ______ ate 18 cookies altogether.
   - (A) Ram, Sumit
   - (B) Aman, Karan
   - (C) Aman, Sumit
   - (D) Ram, Aman

4. ________________ ate 6 cookies more than B.
   - (A) Ram
   - (B) Aman
   - (C) Aayush
   - (D) None of these

Direction (5–7): The picture graph below shows favourite pastimes of a group of children. Study the graph and answer the given questions.

Our Favourite Pastimes				
			▢▢	
▢▢			▢▢	
▢▢		▢▢	▢▢	▢▢
▢	▢▢	▢▢	▢▢	▢▢
	▢			
▢▢		▢▢	▢▢	▢▢
Swimming	Badminton	Tennis	Football	Basket ball

Each ▢ stands for 10 children.

5. If 45 boys like swimming, ________ girls like swimming.
   - (A) 45
   - (B) 35
   - (C) 25
   - (D) Can't say

6. ________________ is the most popular pastime.
   - (A) Badminton
   - (B) Tennis
   - (C) Football
   - (D) Basket ball

7. If the same number of boys and girls like basket ball, __________ boys like basket ball.
   (A) 100 (B) 80
   (C) 60 (D) 30

Direction (8–9) : Use the information below to answer the given questions.

Number of mobile phones sold by Mr. Sharma
Thursday
Friday
Saturday
Sunday

Each stands for 3 mobile phones.

8. He sold __________ mobile phones on Saturday and Sunday.
   (A) 16 (B) 48
   (C) 75 (D) 80

9. If he sold 3 more mobile phones on Friday, he would have sold as many mobile phones as on __________.
   (A) Thursday (B) Saturday
   (C) Sunday (D) None of these

Direction (10–13) : The King's Fun Fair is in town! Children played the games to win tokens and exchange for toys. Read the following information and answer the questions.

Token Exchange Centre		
Toy gun		TOKEN TOKEN TOKEN
Toy aeroplane		TOKEN TOKEN TOKEN TOKEN TOKEN TOKEN
Robot		TOKEN TOKEN TOKEN TOKEN TOKEN TOKEN TOKEN
Teddy bear		TOKEN TOKEN TOKEN TOKEN TOKEN TOKEN TOKEN TOKEN
Mini computer		TOKEN TOKEN TOKEN TOKEN TOKEN TOKEN TOKEN TOKEN TOKEN TOKEN

Each stands for 2 tokens.

10. Shraddha won 10 tokens at the fun fair. She needed __________ more tokens to exchange for a toy robot.
    (A) 1 (B) 2
    (C) 3 (D) 4

11. Golu won twice as many tokens as Shraddha. He could get the __________ .
    (A) Robot
    (B) Teddy bear
    (C) Toy gun
    (D) Mini computer

12. Jasmine had just enough tokens to exchange for a teddy bear. If she wanted to exchange her tokens for a 2 toy aeroplanes, she will need _______ more tokens.
    (A) 8 (B) 6
    (C) 4 (D) 2

13. Krishna won 30 tokens. He exchanged all of them for two toys. He chose the __________ and the ______________ .
    (A) Toy gun, toy plane
    (B) Robot, teddy bear
    (C) Robot, mini computer
    (D) Teddy bear, mini computer

Direction : Look at the picture graph and answer the question.

Numbers of cars in car packing				
1st Floor	2nd Floor	3rd Floor	4th Floor	5th Floor

Each stands for 4 cars

14. There were ______________________ more cars parked on 3rd floor than on the 5th floor.
    (A) 4 (B) 8
    (C) 32 (D) 12

Direction (15–17) : Naina decided to plant trees. So she planted trees for four days.

Monday	🌱🌱🌱🌱
Tuesday	🌱🌱🌱
Wednesday	🌱🌱
Thursday	🌱
Each 🌱 = 2 trees	

Using given information, answer the following.

15. How many tress were planted on Wednesday?
    (A) 8   (B) 10
    (C) 2   (D) 4

16. How many trees were planted on second day?
    (A) 6   (B) 4
    (C) 8   (D) 12

17. How many more trees were planted on Monday than Tuesday?
    (A) 4   (B) 2
    (C) 20   (D) 7

Direction (18–20) : The pictograph shows the number of stickers achieved by four children in a week. Study the graph and answer the following questions.

Shubham	🙂 🙂 🙂 🙂
Aman	🙂 🙂
Lakshya	🙂 🙂 🙂 🙂 🙂
Deepanshu	🙂 🙂 🙂
Each 🙂 = 4 stickers	

18. Who got maximum stickers?
    (A) Shubham   (B) Aman
    (C) Lakshya   (D) Deepanshu

19. Shubham got __________ more stickers than Aman.
    (A) 8   (B) 10
    (C) 9   (D) 15

20. Aman and Deepanshu got __________ stickers altogether.
    (A) 15   (B) 20
    (C) 10   (D) 25

HOTS (ACHIEVERS SECTION)

21. Ankit makes pictograph of the number of toys his friends have. How many less toys Kriti has than the total number of toys 3 friends have?

Sahil	⚪ ⚪
Kriti	⚪ ⚪ ⚪
Pooja	⚪ ⚪ ⚪ ⚪ ⚪
Nihal	⚪ ⚪ ⚪ ⚪ ⚪ ⚪ ⚪
Key : 1⚪ = 2 toys	

    (A) 20   (B) 32
    (C) 24   (D) 26

22. The picture graph shows the number of students present from Monday to Friday.

Monday	🧍 🧍 🧍 🧍
Tuesday	🧍 🧍 🧍
Wednesday	🧍 🧍 🧍 🧍 🧍 🧍
Thursday	🧍 🧍 🧍 🧍
Friday	🧍 🧍
Each 🧍 = 10 students	

How many more students were present on Wednesday than Friday?

(A) 40   (B) 50

(C) 45   (D) 35

23. If

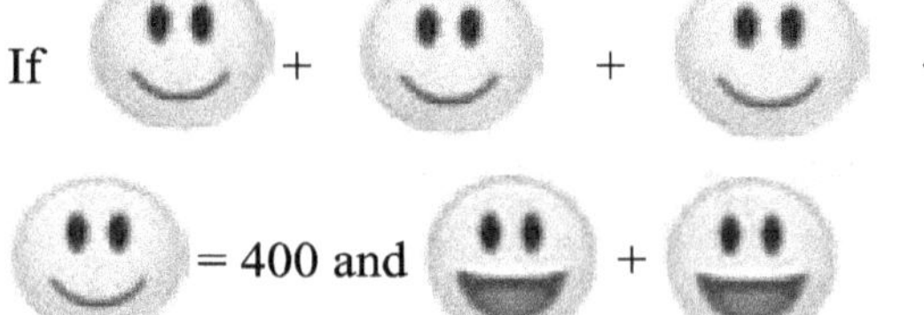

(A) 150   (B) 250

(C) 300   (D) 350

24. The picture graph shows the numbers of pencils purchased by 4 children.

Ram	(pencils)
Shyam	(pencils)
John	(pencils)
Rock	(pencils)
Each	= 10 Pencils

If the cost of one pencil is ₹ 10. How much will Ram have to pay for his pencils?

(a) 300   (b) 400

(c) 500   (d) 600

25. The following pictograph shows the number of balls purchased by 4 girls.

Sony	(balls)
Nisha	(balls)
Priya	(balls)
Jyoti	(balls)
1	= 5 Balls

Using the given information, find out which of the following statements is incorrect?

(A) Sony purchased maximum balls.

(B) Priya purchased 10 balls.

(C) Nisha and Jyoti purchased the same number of balls.

(D) Nisha purchased 5 less balls than Sony.

LOGICAL REASONING

LEARNING OBJECTIVES

- Concept of Analogy
- Concept of Classification
- Length
- Weight
- Time
- Basics of Ranking
- Embedded Figures
- Coding and Decoding

MULTIPLE CHOICE QUESTIONS

1.

(A)   (B)   (C)   (D)

(A)   (B)   (C)   (D)

2.

(A)   (B)   (C)   (D)

3.

4.

(A)   (B)   (C)   (D)

5.

OLYMPIAD WORKBOOK (IMO) CLASS – 2

(A) 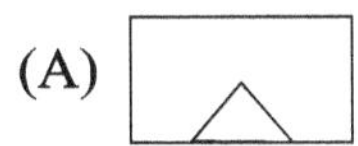   (B) 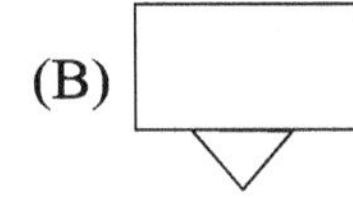

(C) 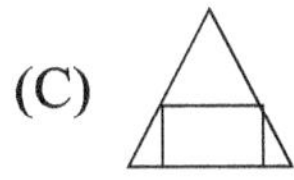   (D) 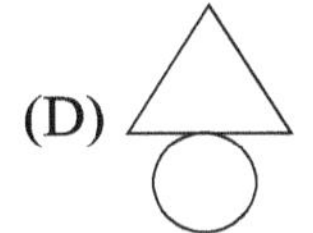

6. (A)    (B)

(C)   (D)

7. (A)   (B)

(C)   (D)

8. (A)   (B)

(C)   (D)

9. (A) April   (B) February
(C) November   (D) September

10. (A)   (B)

(C)   (D)

11. Which fruit is the heaviest?

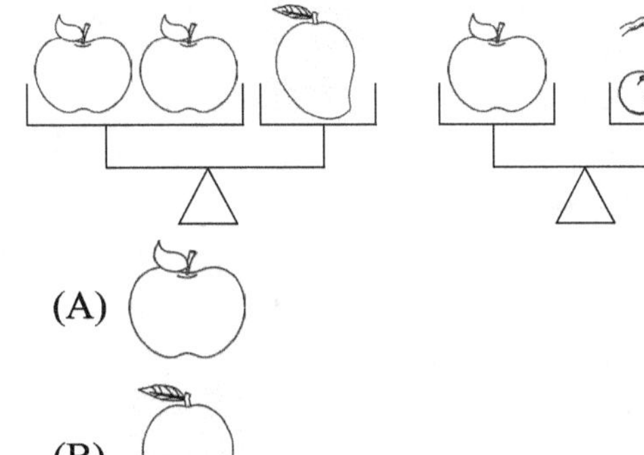

(A)

(B)

(C) 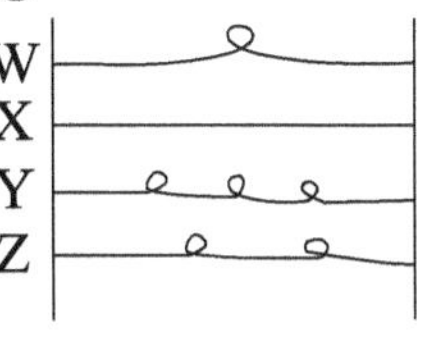

(D) Can't be determined

12. Which string is shortest?

(A) X   (B) W
(C) Z   (D) Y

13. Which tube has maximum capacity?

(A) Q   (B) R
(C) P   (D) S

14. How much is the total given money?

(A) 160   (B) 167
(C) 150   (D) 175

15. Which is the longest pen?

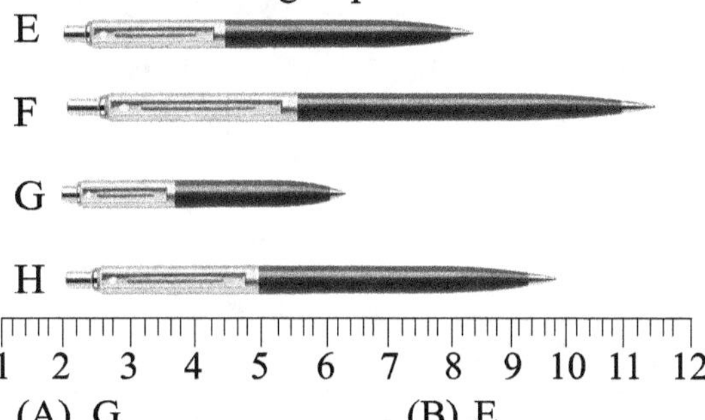

(A) G   (B) E
(C) F   (D) H

16. Which flag is 2nd from the right end?
    (A) Q
    (B) V
    (C) S
    (D) W

17. ___________ is fourth from right end?
    (A) S
    (B) U
    (C) P
    (D) T

18. Which flag is between flag R and Flag T?
    (A) P
    (B) U
    (C) S
    (D) W

19. Which flag is fourth from right and fifth from left end?
    (A) P   (b) W
    (C) T   (D) S

20. If we make one more flag in row after Flag W, then which flag is in the middle of row?
    (A) P   (B) Q
    (C) R   (D) T

21.

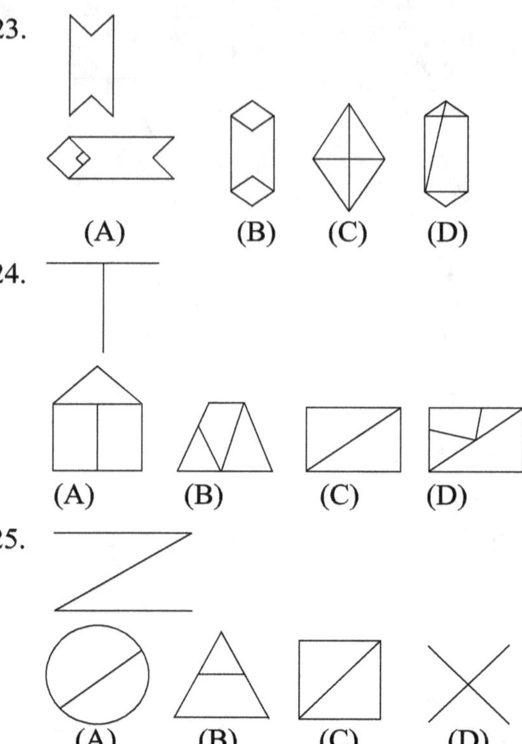

    (A)   (B)   (C)   (D)

22.

    (A)   (B)   (C)   (D)

23.
    (A)   (B)   (C)   (D)

24.
    (A)   (B)   (C)   (D)

25.
    (A)   (B)   (C)   (D)

26. If 'Potato' is called 'Tomato'. 'Tomato' is called 'Radish', 'Radish' is called 'Onion', then the colour of which vegetable is Red.
    (A) Potato
    (B) Radish
    (C) Tomato
    (D) Onion

27. If 'Sky' is called 'Sea', 'Sea' is called 'Water' 'Water' is called 'Air'. 'Air' is called 'Cloud', then what do we drink when thirsty?
    (A) Sky
    (B) Water
    (C) Air
    (D) Cloud

28. If 'Circle' is called 'Square' 'Square' is called 'Triangle'. 'Triangle' is called 'Line segment', then which shape has four sides?
    (A) Circle
    (B) Square
    (C) Triangle
    (D) None of these

29. If 'Tiger' is called 'Cow', 'Cow' is called 'Butterfly' then who eats flesh?
   (A) Tiger
   (B) Cow
   (C) Butterfly
   (D) None of these

30. If 'Water' is called 'Blue', 'Blue' is called 'Red', 'Red' is called 'White', 'White' is called 'Sky' then which of following is the colour of milk?
   (A) Blue   (B) Red
   (C) White   (D) Sky

MODEL TEST PAPER

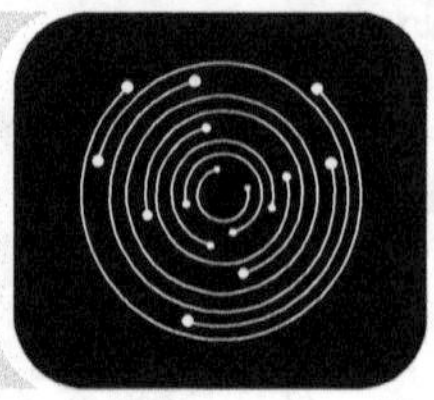

MULTIPLE CHOICE QUESTIONS

1. If L means minus, A means 5, B means 3, then A L B = ?
   (A) 2
   (B) 5
   (C) 0
   (D) None of these

2. In which direction X has to move to reach the given position?

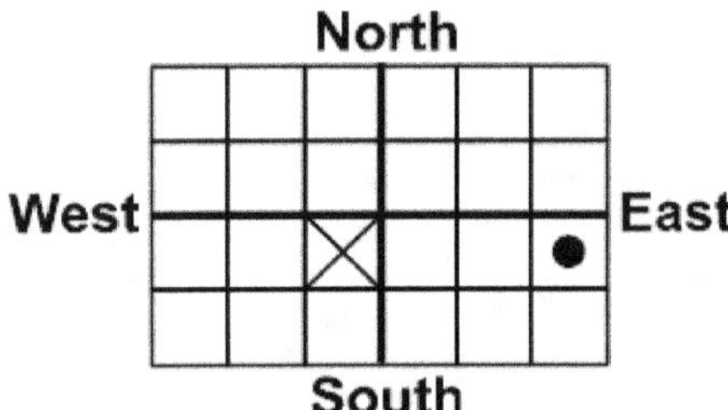

   (A) East   (B) West
   (C) North   (D) South

3. Which day comes after Tuesday?
   (A) Monday   (B) Sunday
   (C) Wednesday   (D) Friday

4. Shraddha had four ₹ 5 coins. She exchanged her money with some notes. If she got 2 notes, which figure shows the amount she got?

   (A) 

   (B) 

   (C) 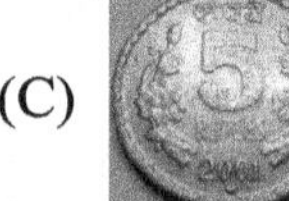  

   (D) 

5. Shubhra has fifty ₹ 2 coins. If she puts them one over the other which geometrical figure will she get?

   (A)   (B)

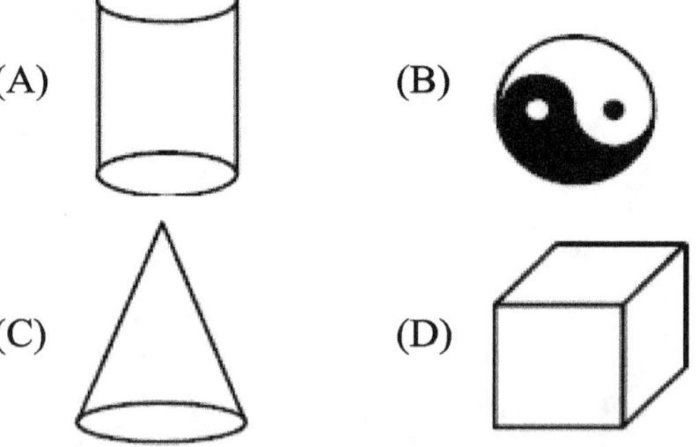

   (C)   (D)

6. Which of the following options shows the number, three greater than the given house number?

   (A) 273   (B) 276
   (C) 275   (D) 277

7. Look at the given pattern:

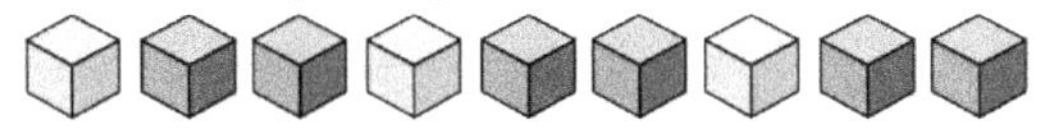

How would you show this pattern using letters?

(A) ABB   (B) ABA
(C) ABC   (D) AAB

8. A fish rod has a code which is used to catch the fish of the same code. Which figure shows the fish, which can be picked by the given fishing rod?

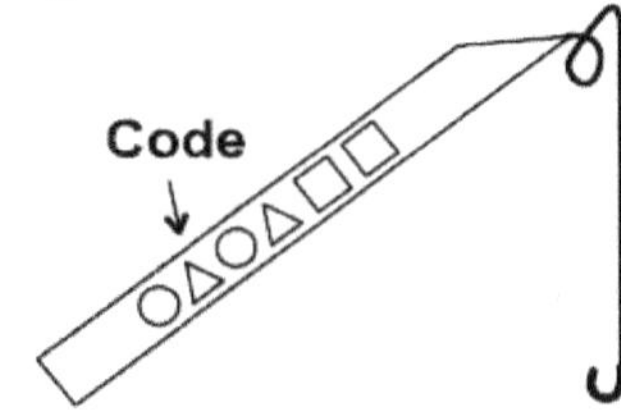

(A) 

(B) 

(C) 

(D) 

9. Toothbrush is longer than pin by __________

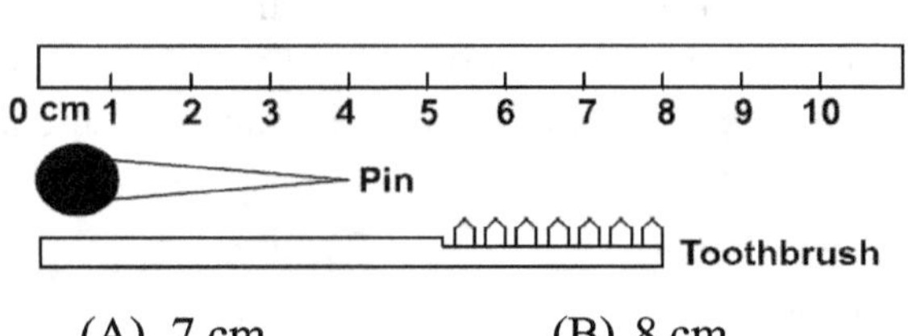

(A) 7 cm   (B) 8 cm
(C) 4 cm   (D) 2 cm

10. Which alphabet belongs to rectangle, circle and triangle?

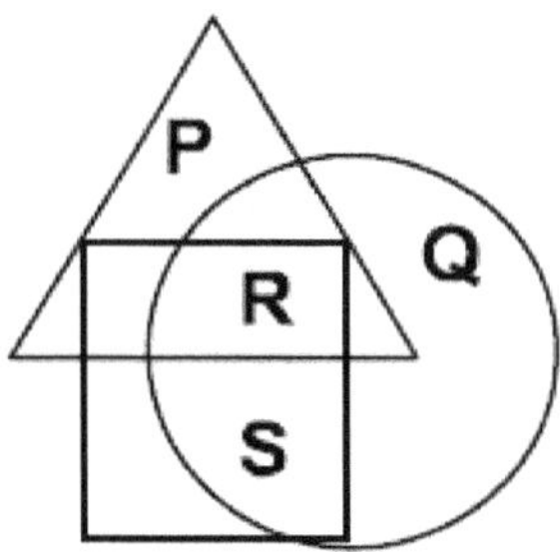

(A) P   (B) Q
(C) R   (D) S

Section II : Mathematical Reasoning

11. Four friends have some playing cards.

Shraddha has a card 2 and said I have an even number.

Golu has a card 3 and said I have an even number.

Ankit has a card 4 and said I have an odd number.

Sheetal has a card 5 and said I have an even number.

Who is right?

(A) Shraddha   (B) Golu
(C) Ankit   (D) Sheetal

12. In a race a student who completes the race in minimum time is the winner. Given below is the time taken by four students W, X , Y and Z to complete a race. Who is the winner?

X: 2 Mins   Y: 180 Sec
Z: 2 Mins 30 Sec   W: 210 Sec

(A) W   (B) X
(C) Y   (D) Z

13. Three friends M, N and O are sitting together. M is taller than N and N is taller than O. Who is the tallest?

(A) M   (B) N
(C) O   (D) Cannot say

14. The numbers that have 2,4,6,8 and 0 in the one's place are called even numbers. Using the information given above find which of the following is even?
(A) 2456
(B) 2520
(C) 7858
(D) All of these

15. Find the position of  in the grid.

(A) Bottom left
(B) Centre
(C) Top centre
(D) Left centre

16. Which of the following is the heaviest?
(A) 1 kg cotton
(B) 1 kg wool
(C) 1 kg iron
(D) All are of the same weight

17. Which of the following figures can be made using four matchsticks?
(A) Circle
(B) Triangle
(C) Square
(D) None of these

18. The cost of three items are given below. Who has enough free money to buy all these items?

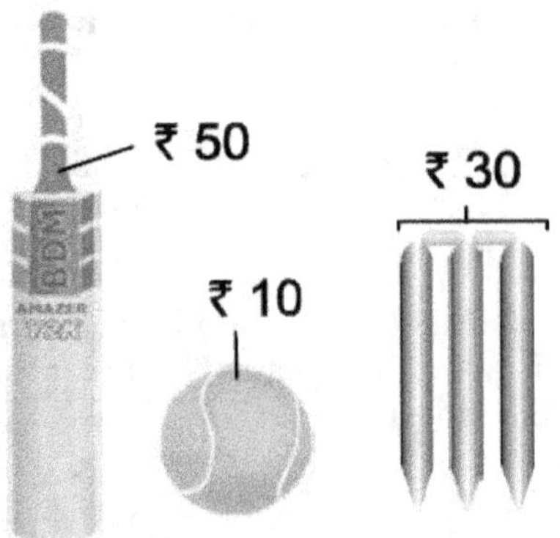

(A) Golu

(B) Ashu

(C) Mehul

(D) Mohan

19. In a city when temperature reaches 5°C snowfall starts. In which city snowfall is going on?
(A) Jammu : 10°C
(B) Leh : 4°C
(C) Delhi : 14°C
(D) Mumbai : 12°C

20. What temperature is shown by the thermometer?

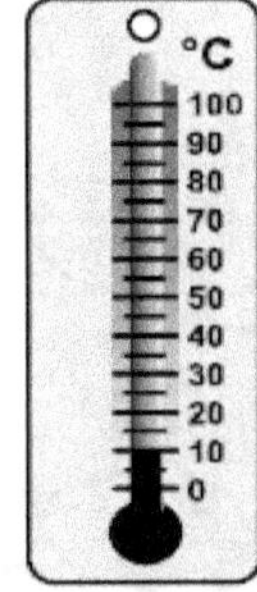

(A) 10°C
(B) 15°C
(C) 20°C
(D) 13°C

Section III : Everyday Mathematics

21. A hotel is 12 meters tall and apartment building is 2 meters taller than the hotel. How many meters tall is the apartment building?
(A) 14 m
(B) 24 m
(C) 20 m
(D) 12 m

22. A shopkeeper bought 340 eggs. Out of them 100 eggs were broken. How many unbroken eggs did the shopkeeper have?

(A) 204   (B) 240
(C) 304   (D) 300

23. Ayush has 5 bunch of bananas. Each bunch has 3 bananas. How many bananas does he have?

(A) 75   (B) 15
(C) 10   (D) 12

24. If a student scoring 8 out of 10 marks gets an A grade, then which among the following will also get an A grade?

(A) 7 out of 10   (B) 5 out of 10
(C) 10 out of 10   (D) 6 out of 10

25. Eight mangoes are shared equally among 2 friends. Each friend will get how many mangoes?

(A) 4   (B) 5
(C) 2   (D) 3

26. I have 10 toffees. I gave two toffees to Priya. I am left with ________ toffees.

(A) 8   (B) 9
(C) 7   (D) 5

27. Ali has 53 marbles. He has 8 more marbles than Henry. If Ali gives 6 marbles to Henry, how many marbles does Henry have now?

(A) 51   (B) 45
(C) 59   (D) 48

28. Mrs. Mehra bought 20 sweets. She wanted her 3 children to share the sweets equally. However, she realised they could not share the sweets equally. What was the greatest number of sweets that each child could receive?

(A) 6   (B) 7
(C) 8   (D) 9

29. Ashu started fixing a broken table at 2:30 p.m. If he took 3 hours 10 minutes to fix the broken table, at what time did he finish?

2.30 p.m.

(A) 6:30 pm   (B) 4:40 pm
(C) 5:30 pm   (D) 5:40 pm

30. Mr. Kapoor had some apples. He gave 13 apples to his son and 16 apples to his daughter. He had 11 apples left. How many apples did he have at first?

(A) 40   (B) 7
(C) 14   (D) 28

Section IV : Achievers Section

31. Shraddha measured the height of a table. She also measured the height of a door. The height of the table was 25 cm shorter than the height of the door. If the height of the door was 150 cm, what was the height of the table?

(A) 125 cm   (B) 175 cm
(C) 135 cm   (D) 185 cm

32. The weight of Anju and Soni is 93 kg. If the weight of Soni is 31 kg, how much heavier is Anju than Soni?

(A) 31 kg   (B) 93 kg
(C) 62 kg   (D) 124 kg

33. Shubhra and Shraddha went shopping and they bought some things. What is the total cost of these things?

(A) ₹ 130   (B) ₹ 145
(C) ₹ 185   (D) ₹ 135

34. One morning, Ashu saw that out of 70 birds only 24 were left. The rest had gone away. How many birds had gone away?

(A) 94 (B) 56

(C) 64 (D) 46

35. Micky collects sticks from the jungle. He sells them in the market. He uses 14 sticks to make 1 bundle. How many sticks will 6 bundles have?

(A) 20 (B) 60

(C) 42 (D) 84

1.	Ⓐ Ⓑ Ⓒ Ⓓ	8.	Ⓐ Ⓑ Ⓒ Ⓓ	15.	Ⓐ Ⓑ Ⓒ Ⓓ	22.	Ⓐ Ⓑ Ⓒ Ⓓ	29.	Ⓐ Ⓑ Ⓒ Ⓓ
2.	Ⓐ Ⓑ Ⓒ Ⓓ	9.	Ⓐ Ⓑ Ⓒ Ⓓ	16.	Ⓐ Ⓑ Ⓒ Ⓓ	23.	Ⓐ Ⓑ Ⓒ Ⓓ	30.	Ⓐ Ⓑ Ⓒ Ⓓ
3.	Ⓐ Ⓑ Ⓒ Ⓓ	10.	Ⓐ Ⓑ Ⓒ Ⓓ	17.	Ⓐ Ⓑ Ⓒ Ⓓ	24.	Ⓐ Ⓑ Ⓒ Ⓓ	31.	Ⓐ Ⓑ Ⓒ Ⓓ
4.	Ⓐ Ⓑ Ⓒ Ⓓ	11.	Ⓐ Ⓑ Ⓒ Ⓓ	18.	Ⓐ Ⓑ Ⓒ Ⓓ	25.	Ⓐ Ⓑ Ⓒ Ⓓ	32.	Ⓐ Ⓑ Ⓒ Ⓓ
5.	Ⓐ Ⓑ Ⓒ Ⓓ	12.	Ⓐ Ⓑ Ⓒ Ⓓ	19.	Ⓐ Ⓑ Ⓒ Ⓓ	26.	Ⓐ Ⓑ Ⓒ Ⓓ	33.	Ⓐ Ⓑ Ⓒ Ⓓ
6.	Ⓐ Ⓑ Ⓒ Ⓓ	13.	Ⓐ Ⓑ Ⓒ Ⓓ	20.	Ⓐ Ⓑ Ⓒ Ⓓ	27.	Ⓐ Ⓑ Ⓒ Ⓓ	34.	Ⓐ Ⓑ Ⓒ Ⓓ
7.	Ⓐ Ⓑ Ⓒ Ⓓ	14.	Ⓐ Ⓑ Ⓒ Ⓓ	21.	Ⓐ Ⓑ Ⓒ Ⓓ	28.	Ⓐ Ⓑ Ⓒ Ⓓ	35.	Ⓐ Ⓑ Ⓒ Ⓓ

HINTS AND SOLUTIONS

1. NUMBER SENSE

Answer Key

1. (B)	2. (D)	3. (B)	4. (D)	5. (C)	6. (D)	7. (A)	8. (B)	9. (D)	10. (B)
11. (D)	12. (D)	13. (A)	14. (A)	15. (C)	16. (A)	17. (C)	18. (D)	19. (C)	20. (C)

1. (B)
Here 925 is greatest 3-digit odd number.

4. (B)
The smallest 3-digit even number is 250.

6. (D)
Required number = 3 2 5

            Ones place
          Tens place
       Hundreds place

7. (A)
Since 432 is greater than 318.
$\therefore$ 432 > 318.

10. (B)
We know the smallest 3-digit number is 100.

13. (A)
Greatest even number formed by the digits 3, 2, 1, is 32.

14. (A)

Predecessor of 390 ⇨ 390 − 1
              ⇨ 389

15. (C)
First no. from right is 8
$\therefore$ Fifth number from right is 2

16. (A)
According to given information
Ones place = 5
Tens place = hundred place + 7
= 1 + 7 = 8
(let)
Hence, required answer is (185).

18. (D)
Clearly, 689 is biggest number.
As the number is formed from three different digits.
$\therefore$ Required number = 8

HOTS (ACHIEVERS SECTION)

21. (C)	22. (D)	23. (D)	24. (A)	25. (C)

2. ADDITION AND SUBTRACTION

Answer Key

1. (D)	2. (A)	3. (A)	4. (A)	5. (A)	6. (D)	7. (C)	8. (D)	9. (A)	10. (A)
11. (A)	12. (B)	13. (D)	14. (A)	15. (C)	16. (B)	17. (A)	18. (D)	19. (D)	20. (B)

1. **(D)**
   $\because 999 + 1 = 1000$
   Hence, 1 must be added to 999 to get 1000.

5. **(A)**
   Putting ? = 4, we get

   $$\begin{array}{r} 5\quad4 \\ +\quad 3\quad8 \\ \hline 9\quad2 \\ \hline \end{array}$$

   Hence, ? = 4

6. **(D)**
   Required result
   $= 9 \times 10 + 5 \times 100 + 3 \times 1$
   $= 90 + 500 + 3 = 593$

8. **(D)**
   If x is the required number, then
   $x + 6 = 14 - x$
   $\Rightarrow \quad 2x = 8 \Rightarrow x = 4$

12. **(B)**
   6 tens $- 4 = 6 \times 10 - 4$
   $= 60 - 4 = 56$

14. **(A)**
   Substituting $\square = 6$; $\Delta = 4$, we see
   $\Delta + \square = 4 + 6 = 10$
   and $\square - \Delta = 6 - 4 = 2$.
   Hence, $\Delta = 4$, $\square = 6$

16. **(B)**
   Required amount $= 300 + 260 = ₹\ 560$

17. **(A)**
   Remaining No. of stamps
   $= 630 - 50 = 580$

19. **(D)**
   Cost of 2 books $= 2 \times 25 = 50$

20. **(B)**
   Total students in school
   $= 300$
   Total girls $\qquad = \underline{125}$
   Total no. of boys $\quad = 175$

HOTS (ACHIEVERS SECTION)

21. (A)	22. (C)	23. (B)	24. (C)	25. (D)

3. MULTIPLICATION AND DIVISION

Answer Key

1. (D)	2. (B)	3. (D)	4. (C)	5. (A)	6. (B)	7. (D)	8. (C)	9. (D)	10. (A)
11. (D)	12. (A)	13. (A)	14. (B)	15. (D)	16. (B)	17. (C)	18. (A)	19. (B)	20. (B)

2. **(B)**

The given series is

$$16 \xrightarrow{+4} 20 \xrightarrow{+4} 24 \xrightarrow{+4} 28$$

$$\xrightarrow{+4} \mathbf{32} \xrightarrow{+4} 36 \xrightarrow{+4} 40$$

$$\therefore \ ? = 32$$

3. **(D)**

We have $3 \times 4 = 12$ and $2 \times 4 = 8$

Clearly, $12 - 8 = 4$

8. **(C)**

Total no. of flowers in pots

$$= 5 \times 4 = 20$$

11. **(D)**

We have $\left(\dfrac{27}{3}\right) \times 8 = 9 \times 8 = 72$

13. **(A)**

The pattern of the given series is

$$80 \xrightarrow{\div 2} 40 \xrightarrow{\div 2} 20 \xrightarrow{\div 2} 10$$

$$\therefore \ ? = 10$$

14. **(B)**

$$\frac{3 \text{ tens}}{3} = \frac{3 \times 10}{3} = \frac{30}{3} = 10$$

<table>
<tr><td colspan="5" align="center">HOTS (ACHIEVERS SECTION)</td></tr>
<tr><td>21. (B)</td><td>22. (A)</td><td>23. (C)</td><td>24. (D)</td><td>25. (A)</td></tr>
</table>

4. LENGTH, WEIGHT, CAPACITY AND TEMPERATURE

Answer Key

1. (C)	2. (D)	3. (A)	4. (C)	5. (C)	6. (C)	7. (B)	8. (C)	9. (D)	10. (D)
11. (C)	12. (B)	13. (A)	14. (B)	15. (C)	16. (C)	17. (C)	18. (B)	19. (B)	20. (C)

16. **(C)**

Distance covered by Seema in one hour: 500 m + 350 m + 150 m = 1000 m

Distance left to cover after one hour = 45 m

Hence, distance travelled in one hour = 1000 m

19. **(B)**

Total mass of the packet of milk and orange juice

$$= 432 + 212 + 212 = 856 \text{ g}$$

<table>
<tr><td colspan="5" align="center">HOTS (ACHIEVERS SECTION)</td></tr>
<tr><td>21. (B)</td><td>22. (A)</td><td>23. (C)</td><td>24. (C)</td><td>25. (B)</td></tr>
</table>

Answer Key

1. (B)	2. (D)	3. (A)	4. (C)	5. (C)	6. (A)	7. (B)	8. (D)	9. (D)	10. (A)
11. (B)	12. (C)	13. (C)	14. (D)	15. (A)	16. (B)	17. (C)	18. (D)	19. (A)	20. (B)

3. (A)
The month with neither 31 days nor 30 days is February.

4. (C)
$$135 \text{ hours} = \frac{135}{24} = 5 \text{ days } 15 \text{ hours}$$

7. (B)
1 day = 24 hours
105 hours = 4 days + 9 hours

13. (C)
Praveen needs = 2 × Cost of 1 eraser + cost of 1 ruler
= 2 × 0.25 + 0.50 = 0.50 + 0.50 = ₹ 1

14. (D)
Cost of 2 textbooks = 4 × 2 = 8
Required difference = 10 − 8 = 2
∴ Kuku can buy one pen.

15. (A)
Total amount = 2 × cost of one pen + 3 × cost of 1 correction pen + cost of 1 textbook
= 2 × 2 + 3 × 1 + 4 = 4 + 3 + 4 = 11

HOTS (ACHIEVERS SECTION)

21. (B)	22. (C)	23. (C)	24. (D)	25. (A)

6. GEOMETRICAL SHAPES

Answer Key

1. (A)	2. (D)	3. (C)	4. (A)	5. (A)	6. (B)	7. (B)	8. (A)	9. (A)	10. (A)
11. (A)	12. (A)	13. (A)	14. (B)	15. (A)	16. (A)	17. (B)	18. (C)	19. (B)	20. (D)

HOTS (ACHIEVERS SECTION)

21. (C)	22. (A)	23. (B)	24. (C)	25. (B)

7. PATTERNS

Answer Key

1. (A)	2. (B)	3. (C)	4. (D)	5. (A)	6. (B)	7. (C)	8. (D)	9. (A)	10. (B)
11. (C)	12. (B)	13. (B)	14. (C)	15 .(A)	16. (B)	17. (D)	18. (A)	19. (A)	20. (C)

2. **(B)**

The next shapes are triangles and squares

3. **(C)**

In star A the numbers are

$$3, \quad 7, \quad 11, \quad 15, \quad 19,$$
$$+4 \quad +4 \quad +4 \quad +4$$

So the numbers in star B are

2, 6, 10, 14, 18

5. **(A)**

$$30, \quad 32, \quad 34, \quad \underline{36,} \quad \underline{38,} \quad 40$$
$$+2 \quad +2 \quad +2 \quad +2 \quad +2$$

7. **(C)**

$$27, \quad 24, \quad 21$$
$$-3 \quad -3$$

So next three numbers are

$\underline{18}, \underline{15}, \underline{12}$

11. **(C)**

N ends the first word M A $\underline{N}$

and starts the second word $\underline{N}$ E T

8. PICTOGRAPHS

Answer Key

1. (A)	2. (C)	3. (B)	4. (D)	5. (B)	6. (C)	7. (D)	8. (B)	9. (B)	10. (D)
11. (D)	12. (A)	13. (B)	14. (B)	15. (D)	16. (A)	17. (B)	18. (C)	19. (A)	20. (B)

1. **(A)**

Clearly, E ate the most number of cookies.

2. **(C)**

E ate $= 3 \times 3 = 9$ cookies.

3. **(B)**

B and D ate $= 2 \times 3 + 4 \times 3 = 6 + 12$

$= 18$ cookies altogether.

4. **(D)**

B ate $= 2 \times 3 = 6$ cookies

and D ate $= 4 \times 3 = 12$ cookies

$\therefore$ D ate 6 cookies more then B.

8. **(B)**

Mr. Sharma sold mobile phones on Saturday and Sunday

$= 3 \times 9 + 3 \times 7 = 27 + 21 = 48$

9. **(B)**

Mr. Sharma sold mobile phones on Friday $=$

$6 \times 3 + 3 = 21$

Clearly, correct answer is (B).

HOTS (ACHIEVERS SECTION)

21. (C)	22. (A)	23. (D)	24. (C)	25. (B)

9. LOGICAL REASONING

Answer Key

1. (A)	2. (B)	3. (B)	4. (C)	5. (B)	6. (B)	7. (C)	8. (D)	9. (B)	10. (C)
11. (B)	12. (A)	13. (D)	14. (B)	15. (C)	16. (B)	17. (A)	18. (C)	19. (C)	20. (D)
21. (C)	22. (A)	23. (B)	24. (D)	25. (B)	26. (B)	27. (C)	28. (C)	29. (B)	30. (D)

9. (B)

Months	No. of Days
April	30
February	29
November	30
September	30

10. (C)

Except him all others are in pair.

14. (B)

₹100 + ₹10 + 2 + ₹50 + ₹25

= ₹167

25. (C)

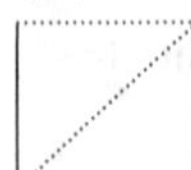

26. (B)

The colour of tomato is red and tomato is called is called Radish.

30. (D)

The color of milk is white and white is called Sky.

MODEL TEST PAPER

Answer Key

1. (A)	2. (A)	3. (C)	4. (A)	5. (A)	6. (B)	7. (A)	8. (A)	9. (C)	10. (C)
11. (A)	12. (B)	13. (A)	14. (D)	15. (B)	16. (C)	17. (C)	18. (A)	19. (B)	20. (A)
21. (A)	22. (B)	23. (B)	24. (C)	25. (A)	26. (A)	27. (A)	28. (A)	29. (D)	30. (A)
31. (A)	32. (A)	33. (D)	34. (D)	35. (D)					

SAMPLE OMR ANSWER SHEET

1. STUDENT NAME (IN ENGLISH CAPITAL LETTERS ONLY)

Students must write and darken the respective circles completely using HB Pencil only. Othewise their Answer Sheets will not be evaluated.

PERSONAL DETAILS

2. SCHOOL CODE

3. CLASS

4. SECTION

5. ROLL NO.

6. QUESTION PAPER SET

A ○
B ○
C ○
D ○

7. MOBILE NUMBER

8. GENDER

MALE ○

FEMALE ○

9. STREAM
(Only for Class XI and XII Students)

MATHEMATICS ○
BIOLOGY ○
OTHERS ○

MARK YOUR ANSWERS

1.	Ⓐ Ⓑ Ⓒ Ⓓ	26.	Ⓐ Ⓑ Ⓒ Ⓓ
2.	Ⓐ Ⓑ Ⓒ Ⓓ	27.	Ⓐ Ⓑ Ⓒ Ⓓ
3.	Ⓐ Ⓑ Ⓒ Ⓓ	28.	Ⓐ Ⓑ Ⓒ Ⓓ
4.	Ⓐ Ⓑ Ⓒ Ⓓ	29.	Ⓐ Ⓑ Ⓒ Ⓓ
5.	Ⓐ Ⓑ Ⓒ Ⓓ	30.	Ⓐ Ⓑ Ⓒ Ⓓ
6.	Ⓐ Ⓑ Ⓒ Ⓓ	31.	Ⓐ Ⓑ Ⓒ Ⓓ
7.	Ⓐ Ⓑ Ⓒ Ⓓ	32.	Ⓐ Ⓑ Ⓒ Ⓓ
8.	Ⓐ Ⓑ Ⓒ Ⓓ	33.	Ⓐ Ⓑ Ⓒ Ⓓ
9.	Ⓐ Ⓑ Ⓒ Ⓓ	34.	Ⓐ Ⓑ Ⓒ Ⓓ
10.	Ⓐ Ⓑ Ⓒ Ⓓ	35.	Ⓐ Ⓑ Ⓒ Ⓓ
11.	Ⓐ Ⓑ Ⓒ Ⓓ	36.	Ⓐ Ⓑ Ⓒ Ⓓ
12.	Ⓐ Ⓑ Ⓒ Ⓓ	37.	Ⓐ Ⓑ Ⓒ Ⓓ
13.	Ⓐ Ⓑ Ⓒ Ⓓ	38.	Ⓐ Ⓑ Ⓒ Ⓓ
14.	Ⓐ Ⓑ Ⓒ Ⓓ	39.	Ⓐ Ⓑ Ⓒ Ⓓ
15.	Ⓐ Ⓑ Ⓒ Ⓓ	40.	Ⓐ Ⓑ Ⓒ Ⓓ
16.	Ⓐ Ⓑ Ⓒ Ⓓ	41.	Ⓐ Ⓑ Ⓒ Ⓓ
17.	Ⓐ Ⓑ Ⓒ Ⓓ	42.	Ⓐ Ⓑ Ⓒ Ⓓ
18.	Ⓐ Ⓑ Ⓒ Ⓓ	43.	Ⓐ Ⓑ Ⓒ Ⓓ
19.	Ⓐ Ⓑ Ⓒ Ⓓ	44.	Ⓐ Ⓑ Ⓒ Ⓓ
20.	Ⓐ Ⓑ Ⓒ Ⓓ	45.	Ⓐ Ⓑ Ⓒ Ⓓ
21.	Ⓐ Ⓑ Ⓒ Ⓓ	46.	Ⓐ Ⓑ Ⓒ Ⓓ
22.	Ⓐ Ⓑ Ⓒ Ⓓ	47.	Ⓐ Ⓑ Ⓒ Ⓓ
23.	Ⓐ Ⓑ Ⓒ Ⓓ	48.	Ⓐ Ⓑ Ⓒ Ⓓ
24.	Ⓐ Ⓑ Ⓒ Ⓓ	49.	Ⓐ Ⓑ Ⓒ Ⓓ
25.	Ⓐ Ⓑ Ⓒ Ⓓ	50.	Ⓐ Ⓑ Ⓒ Ⓓ

Signature of the Student & Date of Examination

Signature of the Invigilator & Date of Examination